Volume 14

make it yourself
The Complete Step-by-Step Library of Needlework and Crafts

COLUMBIA HOUSE/New York

Editor: Mary Harding
Assistant Editor: Margo Coughtrie
Editorial Assistants: Sally Fisher/Maureen Paton
Consultants: Greta Barrett/Angela Jeffs (Sewing)/
Patsy North (Embroidery and Crafts)/
Frances Rogers (Knitting and Crochet)
Managing Editor: Nicholas Wright
Design Co-ordinator: Jan Churcher
Production Control: Sheila Biddlecombe
Editorial Director: Graham Donaldson

© 1973/4/5/6 by Orbis-Verlag für Publizistik GMBH and Co. KG.
© 1975/6/7 Phoebus Publishing Company / BPC Publishing Ltd.

Distributed by Columbia House, 51 West 52nd Street, New York, New York 10019

Printed in U.S.A.

Introduction

In Volume 14, we begin with a selection of knits in the neutral shades—creams, browns, and greys—before bursting into full color with our embroidered, beribboned Bavarian-style jackets. There are lots of striped clothes for the children, too. They'll love wearing them as much as you'll enjoy knitting them.

Our crochet section blossoms out in this volume—quite literally. You can make a net shawl covered with bright blooms or a set of cushions strewn with little flowers and leaves. For you and the family, there are designs for multi-colored pullovers. Loop crochet, which produces an interesting textured pile, is introduced as a new technique.

Whether you feel like treating yourself to a glamorous evening dress or making some rough-and-tumble clothes for the children, you'll find a suitable pattern in the dressmaking section. For those who can't resist bags, we present a selection in strong canvas.

Moving on to embroidery, there are some bead patterns to stitch onto fabric—the effect is brilliant. We end on a floral note with painted flower arrangements and découpage.

make it yourself

Contents   Page

How to use this book Body measurements chart   **1672-1673**
                         Fashion sizing
                         Metric conversion
                         Selecting a yarn

Knitting   How-to instructions   **1675-1705**
                         Boleros
                         Cardigans
                         Dresses
                         Jackets
                         Pullovers
                         Shawl
                         Skirts
                         Tank tops
                         Vest

Crochet   How-to instructions   **1706-1721**
                         Jackets
                         Pillows
                         Place mats
                         Pullovers
                         Scarf
                         Shawl

Dressmaking   How-to instructions   **1722-1743**
                         Bathrobes
                         Children's clothes
                         Culottes
                         Evening dresses
                         Jackets
                         Pants
                         Shirts
                         Skirts

Sewing   How-to instructions   **1744-1763**
                         Back pack
                         Bags
                         Carry-alls
                         Denim designs
                         Dungarees
                         Jackets
                         Nightgowns
                         Pillow dolls
                         Skirt

Embroidery   Embroidery pattern   **1762-1766**
                         Skirt

Crafts   How-to instructions   **1767-1786**
                         Beaded alphabet monograms
                         Beaded bags
                         Beaded belt
                         Craft patterns
                         Decorative duck
                         Découpage
                         Floral display
                         Painted flowers

Index   **1787-1788**

Notes   **1789-1792**

How to use this book..

Selecting a yarn

In this series, we are introducing a new and easy way to identify the yarn used in our knitting and crochet features! You will find an actual-size, colored photograph of the yarn given with each set of directions.

Materials Required:

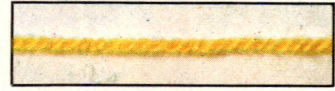

150 (200) gm or 6 (7) oz each of yellow and green, 50 gm or 2 oz blue [100 gm = 360 m or 390 yds]. Knitting needles size 4 (Am) or 10 (Eng).

At one time or another, you have probably suffered the disappointment of finding that the yarn specified in knitting and crochet directions is difficult to obtain or totally unavailable in your area. When this happens you are faced with the often impossible task of finding a substitute yarn. By matching a yarn against our photograph, you can choose a yarn of similar weight and texture from the range of yarns available in your store or favorite needlework shop.

This method is also helpful if you have yarn left over from other projects and you are unsure whether it is the proper weight or texture and whether you have sufficient yardage to finish a new shawl or pullover.

To help you determine the amount of yarn needed, we have also listed the yardage per skein for the yarn used. Most yarn companies give the yardage per skein in their sample books, and many shops have interchangeable yarn lists which give the yardages per unit weight. You will then be able to see whether you will need to make adjustments in the number of skeins required of the yarn which you have chosen.

Before you start to work the pattern, work a test swatch and match it against the Tension given in the directions (see the Tension Gauge instructions below). Adjust the needle or hook size if necessary. Any yarn which can be worked at the tension given in the directions can be used for that pattern.

Centimeters or inches?

The metric system of measurement is gaining greater use and acceptance, and some needlework and crafts equipment and materials are already sold by the metric weight and/or length. For your convenience, we have given all the weights and measures in both systems. <u>NOTE</u>: In some cases, the conversions are not exact. The measurements have been rounded to the nearest convenient or appropriate number.

Tension gauge

One key to successful knitting or crocheting is the tension! Each of our directions is based on the given tension gauge (number of rows and stitches to 10 cm or 4″).

To check your tension, work a test piece 12 cm or 5″ square in the stitch pattern. Make a cardboard template with a 10 cm or 4″ square cut out of it. Place the template over your swatch and count the rows and stitches. Compare the numbers with the tension gauge given in the directions. If your swatch has too few stitches and rows, work more tightly or use smaller equipment. If you have more than the number given, use larger needles, or hook. Directions for the items shown can be used for any yarn of similar thickness and texture, providing you can achieve the proper tension.

Do not be upset if you find that you do have to adjust the needle or hook size. This does not mean that there is anything wrong with your knitting or crocheting. The needle and hook sizes given in the directions are an average, but by no means an absolute. There is great variation in the tension at which different people work, and you will even find slight variations in the tension of your work. On days when you are tense or tired, your knitting or crocheting will probably be a little tighter.

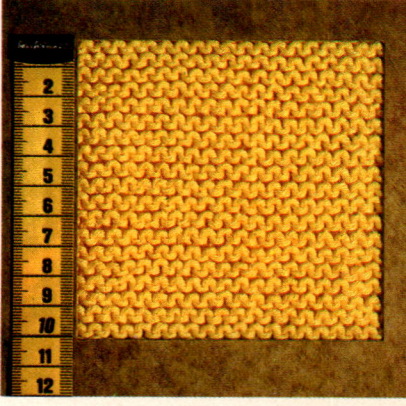

Fashion sizing

Dressmaking

Do you know your size? Don't just say 'yes', because as you already know, the fit of pattern and ready-to-wear sizes varies.

To eliminate confusion, we have lettered our sizes (A, B, C) instead of giving them the traditional numbering (10, 12).

Remeasure yourself and match your body measurements with those given in the chart below. All of the patterns are designed according to these measurements, so choose the pattern size which is right for your measurements. You may have to make minor adjustments in the pattern pieces to adapt them to your body contours, and Dressmaking Pattern Sheet 2 explains how to do this. Other dressmaking pattern sheets will deal with more complex fitting for specific garments such as pants.

DO NOT MEASURE THE PATTERNS. Every pattern includes, according to the design, an added measure to allow for easy movement when wearing the garment. Just compare your body measurements with the measurements given in the chart and choose the proper size.

Each pattern is given in five sizes. Two of the sizes are given on the pattern sheet and the other three sizes can be easily drawn from the two sizes given. Directions for adapting for the three additional sizes are given on each pattern sheet. Even if you are not one of the standard pattern sizes, but are a mixed size made up of several standard measurements, you can still use our patterns. Since each pattern can be adapted for five sizes – a size smaller, a size larger, and a size between the two sizes actually marked on the pattern sheet – it is possible to construct a pattern for yourself. Directions for constructing a mixed-size pattern are given on Dressmaking Pattern Sheet 2.

Do you know your size?

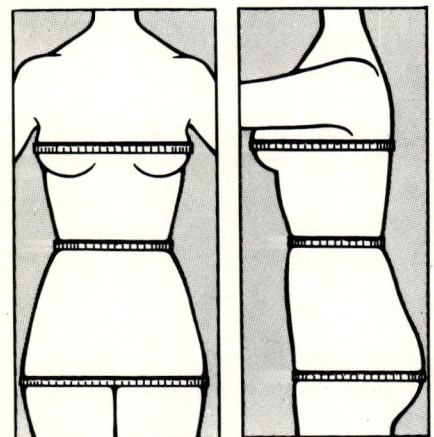

Don't just say 'yes'. Remeasure yourself, following the diagrams and instructions, and then check the Body Measurements chart.

Bust – measure around the fullest part of the bust.

Waist – tie a string around your body so that it settles comfortably at your natural waistline. Measure your waist at the string.

Hips – measure around the fullest part of your hips (this generally falls 7″–9″ below your waistline).

Important hints:

When taking measurements, do not hold the tape measure slack or pull it too tight. The tape must lie evenly horizontal all around the body – it should not go up at the back and down at the front. You will find it simpler and more accurate to be measured by someone else.

Knitting and Crochet

The knitting and crochet sizes are based on the Dressmaking Body Measurements Chart. For each direction, you will be given the actual body measurements for which the garment is intended. The finished knitted or crocheted garment will be larger than the given measurements to allow for comfort and movement.

Size: Directions are for 92 cm (36″) bust. Changes for 96, 100 cm (37½″, 39½″) bust are in brackets.

Body measurements chart

WOMEN

Size	A	B	C	D	E	F	G	H
Bust	80 cm (31½″)	84 cm (33″)	88 cm (34½″)	92 cm (36″)	96 cm (37½″)	100 cm (39½″)	104 cm (41″)	108 cm (42½″)
Waist	59 cm (23¼″)	63.5 cm (25″)	68 cm (26½″)	72.5 cm (28½″)	77 cm (30½″)	81.5 cm (32″)	86 cm (34″)	90 cm (35½″)
Hips	86 cm (34″)	90 cm (35½″)	94 cm (37″)	98 cm (38½″)	102 cm (40″)	106 cm (42″)	110 cm (43½″)	114 cm (45″)

MEN

Size	J	K	L	M	N	O	P	Q
Chest	84 cm (33″)	88 cm (34½″)	92 cm (36″)	96 cm (37½″)	100 cm (39½″)	104 cm (41″)	108 cm (42½″)	112 cm (44″)
Hip	88 cm (34½″)	92 cm (36″)	96 cm (37½″)	100 cm (39½″)	104 cm (41″)	108 cm (42½″)	112 cm (44″)	116 cm (45½″)
Neck	36 cm (14″)	37 cm (14½″)	38 cm (15″)	39 cm (15½″)	40 cm (15¾″)	41 cm (16″)	42 cm (16½″)	43 cm (17″)
Arm	60 cm (23¾″)	61 cm (24″)	62 cm (24¼″)	63 cm (24¾″)	64 cm (25¼″)	65 cm (25½″)	66 cm (26″)	67 cm (26½″)

CHILDREN

Size	S	T	U	V	W	X	Y	Z
Height	110 cm (43″)	116 cm (45½″)	122 cm (48″)	128 cm (50½″)	134 cm (52¾″)	140 cm (55″)	146 cm (57½″)	152 cm (60″)
Chest	60 cm (23¾″)	62 cm (24¼″)	64 cm (25¼″)	66 cm (26″)	68 cm (26¾″)	70 cm (27½″)	73 cm (28¾″)	76 cm (29¾″)
Waist	58 cm (23″)	59 cm (23¼″)	60 cm (23¾″)	61 cm (24″)	62 cm (24¼″)	63 cm (24¾″)	64 cm (25¼″)	65 cm (25¾″)
Hips	66 cm (26″)	68 cm (26¾″)	70 cm (27½″)	72 cm (28¼″)	74 cm (29″)	76 cm (29¾″)	80 cm (31½″)	84 cm (33″)

Knitting

Fresh as a summer breeze

This cardigan will be perfect for a boat trip or any outing on a lazy summer afternoon. It has a wide collarless neck, so it can be worn with any style of dress or blouse collar. Deep ribbing at the waist and large patch pockets complete the look.

Knitting

Size: Directions are for 88 cm or 34½" bust. Changes for 96 cm or 37½" bust are in brackets.

Materials Required:

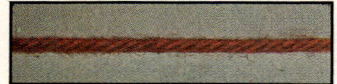

600 (650) gm or 22 (23) oz ecru [50 gm = 140 m or 153 yds]. Knitting needles sizes 1 and 4 (Am) or 9 and 12 (Eng). Circular needle size 1 (Am) or 12 (Eng). 6 buttons.

Basic Pattern (with larger needles): R 1 and 3: P. R 2: K 1, *P 1, K 3, repeat from * to last 2 sts, P 1, K 1. R 4: K 3, *P 1, K 3, repeat from * to last 4 sts, P 1, K 3. These 4 R form the pattern.

Tension: 23 sts and 33 R = 10 cm or 4".

Abbreviations: K = knit. P = purl. St(s) = stitch(es). R = row(s).

DIRECTIONS

Back: Using larger needles, cast on 115 (123) sts and work 2 R in K 1, P 1 rib. Work in Basic Pattern to 8 cm or 3", then decrease 1 st each end of next and every 10th R 4 times — 105 (113) sts. Continue straight to 21 cm or 8¼". Change to smaller needles and work in rib to 29 cm or 11½". Change back to larger needles and continue in Basic Pattern, increasing 1 st each end of every 20th R 2 times — 109 (117) sts. Work to 48 cm or 19".

Shape Armholes: Casting off at beginning of every R, cast off 3 (5) sts 2 times, 2 sts 6 times, and 1 st 6 times. Now decrease 1 st each end of every 4th R 2 times — 81 (85) sts. Work straight to 67 (68) cm or 26½" (26¾").

Shape Shoulder: Cast off 4 (4) sts at beginning of next 6 R and then 4 (5) sts at beginning of next 4 R. *At the same time,* at 68 (69) cm or 26¾" (27¼"), cast off center 31 sts. Work on each side separately. At neck edge, cast off 2 sts at beginning of next 2 R and 1 st on next R.

Left Front: Using larger needles cast on 55 (59) sts; work to match Back for pattern and side, armhole, and shoulder shapings. *At the same time,* when work measures 42 cm or 16½", shape Front edge by decreasing 1 st at beginning of next and every 3rd R 6 times, in every 4th R 5 times, and in every 5th R 6 times.

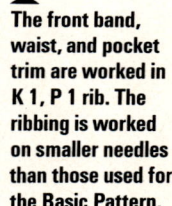

The front band, waist, and pocket trim are worked in K 1, P 1 rib. The ribbing is worked on smaller needles than those used for the Basic Pattern.

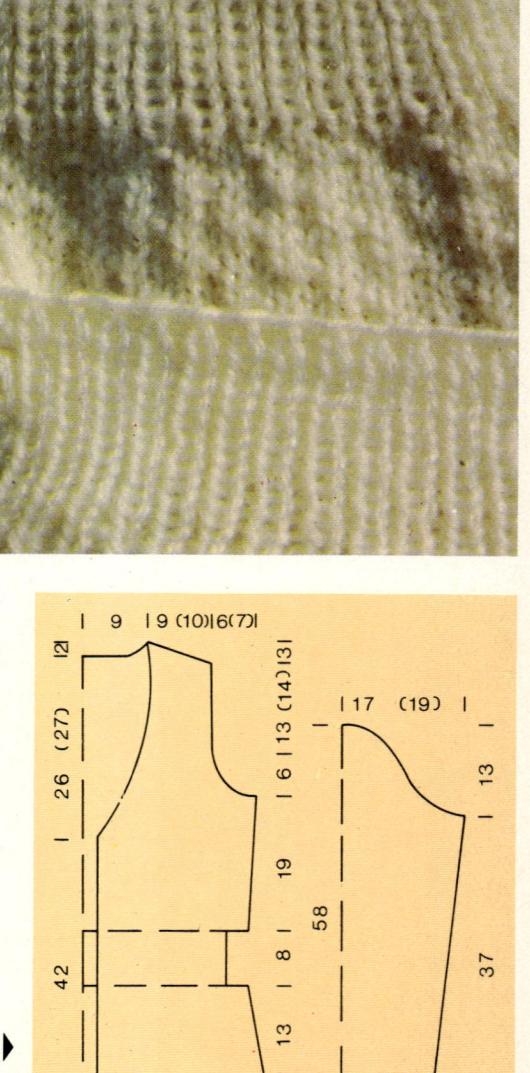

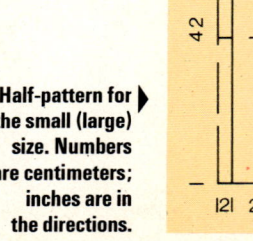

Half-pattern for the small (large) size. Numbers are centimeters; inches are in the directions.

1676

Right Front: Work to match Left Front, reversing shapings.

Sleeves: Using smaller needles, cast on 59 (63) sts and work 8 cm or 3" in K 1, P 1 rib. Change to larger needles and work in Basic Pattern, increasing 1 st each end of every 14th (10th) R 9 (12) times — 77 (87) sts. Work straight to 35 cm or 13¾".

Shape Top: Cast off 4 (7) sts at beginning of next 2 R, 3 sts at beginning of next 4 R, 2 sts at beginning of next 4 R, 1 st at beginning of next 2 R. Now decrease 1 st each end of every 4th R 5 times, decrease 1 st at beginning of next 2 R, 2 sts at beginning of next 4 R, 3 sts at beginning of next 4 R, and 4 (6) sts at beginning of next 2 R. Cast off.

Pockets: Using larger needles, cast on 43 sts and work in Basic Pattern to 13 cm or 5¼". Now work a shortened R, by working fewer sts at end of every 2nd R thus: Work to last 9 sts, pass yarn over needle (to increase a stitch), turn piece, and work to end. Continue, leaving 8 sts more on 2nd R then alternately 9 and 8 sts until 34 sts are left unworked. Change to smaller needles and work across all sts in rib, working the increased st together with the next st through back of st. Work in rib for 4 cm or 1½". Cast off in rib. Work other pocket, reversing shortened R.

Front Band: Using circular needle, cast on 495 sts and work in rib for 2 cm or ¾", working back and forth. In next 2 R, work buttonholes. Cast off 7 sts, beginning at 7th st, then work 5 more at 15 st intervals. In 2nd R, cast on 7 sts at buttonholes and work to 4 cm or 1½". Cast off in rib.

Finishing: Press work. Join all seams. Sew pockets 1 cm or ½" from lower edge and 3 cm or 1" from Front edge. Sew on band and buttons.

How-to

Picot edging

1 Work five rows in stocking or stockinette stitch. In the sixth row, alternately pass the yarn over the needle (to increase one stitch) and knit the next two stitches together.

2 In the following row, purl all of the stitches (including the increased stitches). Work four more rows of stocking or stockinette stitch.

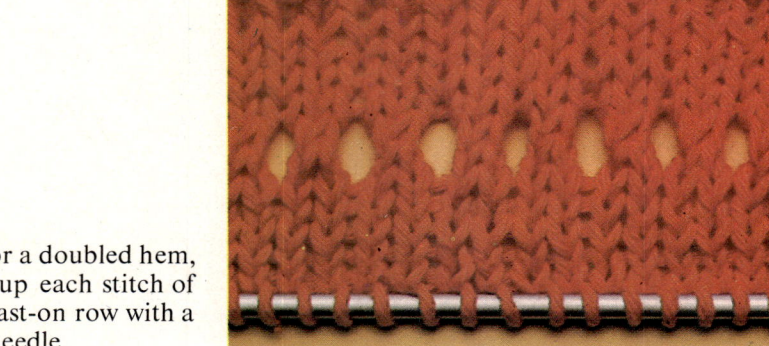

3 For a doubled hem, pick up each stitch of the cast-on row with a fine needle.

4 Place the two needles together and knit the two stitches together (one stitch from each needle). Or alternatively, you can turn the piece with the purl side outside and purl the two rows together.

1677

Quite a catch

Bring back the classics with this white wrap-over jacket. It'll see you through summer and winter alike and will team up with smart or sporty outfits. The intriguing plait pattern covers the whole jacket and will present no problems to the experienced knitter.

Size: Directions are for 96 cm or 37½" bust. Changes for 104 cm or 41" bust are in brackets.

Materials Required:

700 (750) gm or 25 (27) oz white [50 gm = 150 m or 165 yds]. Knitting needles sizes 1 and 2 (Am) or 11 and 12 (Eng). Cable needle. St holders.

Basic Pattern: R 1: (right side) * (K twice in next st, K 1) 4 times, P 6 (7).* Repeat from * to * given number of times. R 2 and wrong side R: * K 6 (7), P 12.* Repeat from * to * given number of times. R 3: *Slip 4 sts onto cable needle and leave at front of work, K 4, then K the 4 sts from cable needle, K 4, P 6 (7).* Repeat from * to * given number of times. R 5 and 7: Work sts as they present themselves. R 9: *K 4, slip next 4 sts onto cable needle and leave at back of work, K next 4 sts, then K 4 sts from cable needle, P 6 (7).* Repeat from * to * given number of times. R 11 and 13: Work sts as they present themselves. R 14: As R 2.
Repeat R 3–14 for the Basic Pattern.

Tension: 36 sts and 38 R = 10 cm or 4".

Abbreviations: K = knit. P = purl. St(s) = stitch(es). R = row(s).

DIRECTIONS

Back: Using finer needles cast on 156 (172) sts and work 4 cm or 1½" in K 2, P 2 rib. Change to thicker needles and place sts thus: R 1: K 1, P 3 (6), then work from * to * of R 1 of Basic Pattern 10 times, (K twice into next st, K 1) 4 times, P 3 (6), K 1 – 200 (216) sts. Continue, working Basic Pattern over main sts (thus having 11 cables). Work straight to 17 cm or 6¾". Next R: K 1, P 1 (4), P 2 together, **pattern 12, P 4 (5), P 2 together, repeat from ** 9 times more, pattern 12, P 3 (P 2 together, P 4), K 1. Work straight with new P strip to 30 cm or 11¾"**.
In next R repeat the last decrease R, but for 1st size decrease in last P rib instead of 1st P rib – 178 (192) sts. Continue straight to 50 (49) cm or 19¾" (19¼").
Shape Armholes: At beginning of every R, cast off 4 (6) sts 2 times, 3 sts 4 times, 2 sts 8 times, and 1 st 8 (10) times – 134 (142) sts. Continue straight to 70 cm or 27½".
Shape Neck and Shoulders: Cast off center 48 sts and work on each side separately. At neck edge, in every 2nd R cast off 2 sts 2 times and 1 st 1 time. At the same time, at armhole edge, in every 2nd R cast off 9 (10) sts 2 times and 10 (11) sts 2 times.
Left Front: Using finer needles, cast on 72 (82) sts and work 4 cm or 1½" in K 2, P 2 rib. Change to thicker needles and place sts as for Back, but repeat from ** to ** 4 times instead of 10 times – 92 (102) sts.
Decrease in P panels, shape armhole and shoulder as for Back, and work straight at front edge to 50 cm or 19¾", ending at front edge.
Shape Front: At beginning of next R, cast off 2 sts 1 time, then in every 4th R, at front edge, decrease 1 st 20 (21) times.
Right Front: Work as for Left Front, reversing all shapings.
Sleeves: Using finer needles, cast on 64 (68) sts and work in K 2, P 2 rib, increasing 1 st at end of last R for 2nd size only – 64 (69) sts. Change to thicker needles and place sts thus: K 1, P 6 (7), then repeat R 1 of Basic Pattern from * to * 4 times, K 1 – 80 (85) sts.
Continue in pattern, increasing 1 st each end of every 4th and 6th R alternately 25 (28) times – 130 (141) sts. Work straight to 45 cm or 17¾".
Shape Top: At beginning of every R, cast off 4 (5) sts 2 times, 3 sts 4 (6) times, 2 sts 38 (34) times, 3 sts 4 (6) times, 4 (5) sts 2 times. Cast off remaining 14 (17) sts.
Roll Collar and Front Band: Using finer needles, cast on 22 sts and work in K 1, P 1 rib to 44 cm or 17¼". R 1: (right edge) Rib 2, work K 1, P 1, K 1 into next st, rib to end. Work 3 R straight. Repeat these 4 R 11 times more. At the same time, at left edge, increase 1 st every 2nd R 28 times – 74 sts. Work straight to 70 cm or 27½", ending at right edge. R 2 and 3: Rib 60 sts, turn and rib back. R 4–7: Work over all sts. Repeat R 2–7 9 times more. Leave sts on st holder. Work another half to match, reversing all shapings, then graft the sts together.
Belt: Using finer needles, cast on 17 sts and work in K 1, P 1 rib for 130 cm or 51". Cast off in rib.
Finishing: Press lightly on wrong side. Join all seams, then sew on Collar and Band.

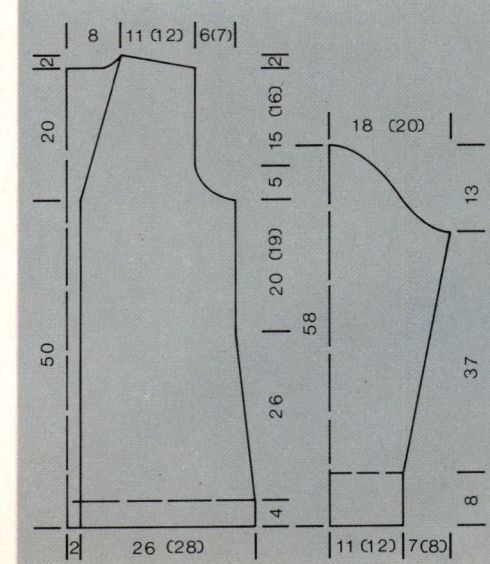

Half-pattern small (large) size. The numbers are centimeters; inches are in the directions.

Knitting

In the Peruvian style

Style 1
This little bolero is in white with simple stripes and bound edges worked in brown yarn.

These designs reflect the current interest in traditional and ethnic influences. The simple bolero shape makes them a perfect finishing touch for a variety of casual outfits. Use bouclé yarn worked in stocking or stockinette stitch throughout.

Size: Directions are for 80 cm or 31½" bust. Changes for 88 cm or 34½" bust are in brackets.

Materials Required:

Bouclé: 100 (150) gm or 4 (6) oz white, 100 gm or 4 oz brown [50 gm = 80 m or 90 yds]. For sewing seams: plain yarn in white and brown. Knitting needles and circular needle size 4 (Am) or 9 (Eng).

Basic Stitch: St st.

Stripe Sequence: (Style 1) 5 R brown; 2 R each white, brown, white; 11 R brown; 2 R each white, brown, white; 5 R brown (33 R).

Knitting Diagram: (Style 2) Each colored cross represents 1 stitch. Work R 1–33 1 time.

Tension: 16 sts and 26 R = 10 cm or 4".

Abbreviations: St(s) = stitches. R = row(s). St st = stocking or stockinette stitch.

DIRECTIONS

Back: Using white, cast on 65 (71) sts and work in Basic Stitch to 20 (21) cm or 8" (8¼").

Shape Armholes: At beginning of every R cast off 5 (3) sts 2 times, 2 sts 6 (8) times, and 1 st 4 times — 39 (45) sts. Work straight to 25 (27) cm or 10" (10½"), then continue in Stripe Sequence or follow Knitting Diagram by beginning R with K 1 for edge st, then work from 1st (7th) st from right edge of repeat to end, work the repeat of 12 sts 2 (3) times, then end st shown on chart and K 1 for edge st. Continue in pattern to 38 (40) cm or 15" (15½").

Shape Neck and Shoulders: Cast off center 13 (17) sts and work on each side separately. On every 2nd R at neck edge cast off 2 sts 1 time and 1 st 1 time. *At the same time,* at armhole edge cast off 3 sts 2 (1) times and 4 sts 1 (2) time(s).

Left Front: Using white, cast on 28 (31) sts and work in Basic Stitch to 20 (21) cm or 8" (8¼").

Shape Armholes and Front Edge: Shape armhole as for Back and decrease 1 st at Front edge on 1st row, then on every 10th (7th) R 4 (6) times. *At the same time,* at 25 (27) cm or 10" (10½") work in Stripe Sequence or follow Knitting Diagram, working edge sts for Knitting Diagram as for Back, and working 1st repeat from 1st (10th) st of chart. At 38 (40) cm or 15" (15½"), shape shoulder as for Back.

Right Front: Work to

Style 2
The basic pattern and colors are the same — only the design is different. The star and stripe design is attractive, but slightly more complicated.

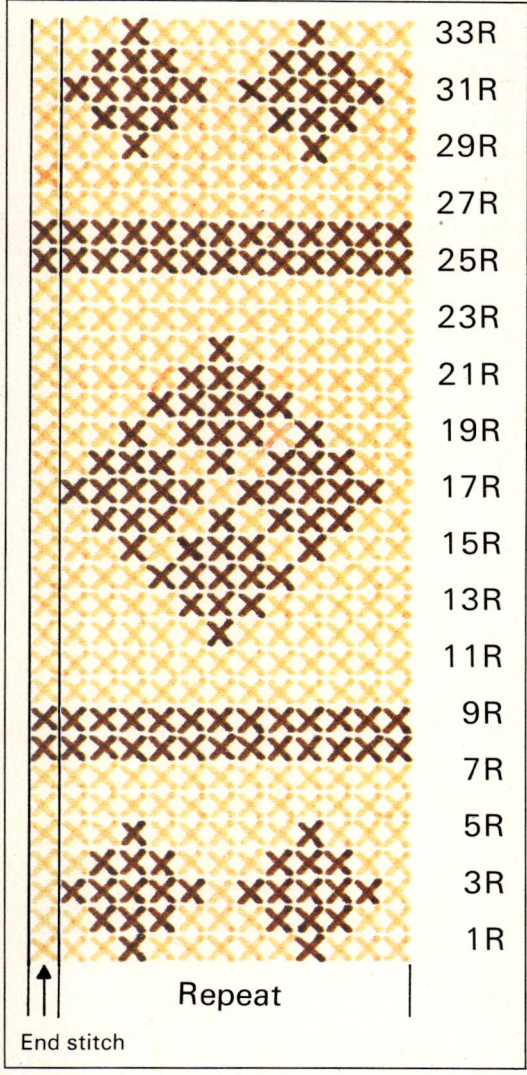

Repeat

End stitch

match Left Front, reversing all shapings.

Armhole Bands: Using brown, cast on 74 (80) sts and work 4 cm or 1½" in st st. Cast off.

Bolero Border: Using circular needle and brown, cast on 274 (298) sts and work back and forth in st st for 4 cm or 1½". Cast off.

Finishing: Pin out parts, cover with damp cloth, and leave to dry. Join all seams, using a medium-weight plain yarn. Sew on Armhole Bands and Bolero Border.

▲ Knitting Diagram: for Style 2. Each colored cross = 1 stitch.

◄ The back shows the two-color pattern to its best advantage.

► Half-pattern for small (large) size. Numbers are centimeters; inches are in the directions.

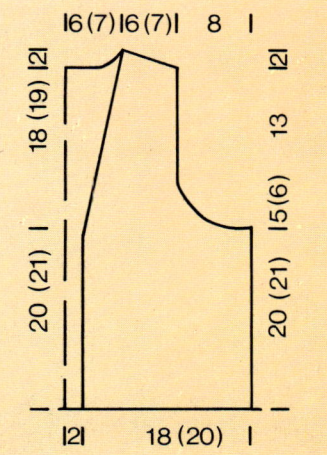

Country stroller in country shades

Knitting

It is unlikely that you have a stole as long, light, and pretty as this one. Made in mohair, you can wrap it around you, not just once but twice.

Size: 250 cm x 70 cm or 99" x 27½".
Materials Required:

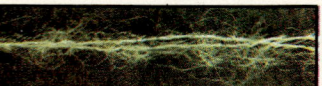

200 gm or 8 oz beige, 150 gm or 6 oz each light and dark brown [25 gm = 106 m or 116 yds]. Knitting needles size 15 (Am) or 00 (Eng).
Basic Pattern: Garter stitch with yarn used double throughout.
Tension: 11 sts and 22 R = 10 cm or 4".
Abbreviations: St(s) = stitch(es). R = row(s).

DIRECTIONS

Using dark brown double, cast on 275 sts and work in Basic Pattern with yarn used double in color sequence thus: * 5 R dark brown, 2 R light brown, 6 R dark brown, 2 R beige, 6 R dark brown, 6 R light brown, 2 R beige, 6 R light brown, 2 R dark brown, 6 R light brown, 6 R beige, 2 R dark brown, 6 R beige, 2 R light brown, 6 R beige, 2 R light brown, 6 R beige, 2 R dark brown, * then 6 R beige — center reached. Then work the stripes from * to * in reverse, thus beginning with 2 R dark brown. After the last 5 R of dark brown, cast off loosely.
Finishing: Cut yarn into 50 cm or 20" lengths and work a knotted fringe into every 2nd R, using 3 strands at a time and working each tassel in colors to match R.

In brown, naturally

Size: Directions are for 84 cm or 33" bust. Changes for 92 cm or 36" bust are in brackets.

Materials Required:

150 (200) gm or 6 (8) oz ecru, 50 gm or 2 oz each beige and brown [50 gm = 115 m or 125 yds]. Knitting needles sizes 2 and 4 (Am) or 9 and 11 (Eng). Circular needle size 2 (Am) or 11 (Eng).

Basic Stitch: St st.

Knitting Diagram: 1 repeat of 8 sts is given.

Color Sequence: *2 R beige, 2 R brown, 10 R of Diagram, 2 R brown, 2 R ecru, 6 R beige, 2 R ecru, 10 R brown, 2 R beige, 2 R ecru, 2 R brown, 6 R beige, 2 R ecru, repeat from *.

Tension: 18 sts and 30 R = 10 cm or 4".

Abbreviations: K = knit. P = purl. St(s) = stitch(es). St st = stocking or stockinette st. R = row(s).

DIRECTIONS

Back: Using finer needles and ecru, cast on 76 (84) sts and work in K 1, P 1 rib for 4 cm or 1½". Change to thicker needles and st st and work in Color Sequence to 10th R. Work R 1 from Knitting Diagram thus: K 1 (edge st), K sts 7–8 1 time, repeat sts 1–8 9 (10) times, K 1 (edge st). Continue in pattern as set, increasing 1 st each end of 11th R and every 16th R 3 times. Keep pattern in line when increasing. Work straight to 30 (31) cm or 11¾" (12¼").

Shape Armholes: At beginning of every R cast off 6 sts 2 times, 2 sts 4 times, 1 st 4 times — 60 (68) sts. Work 4 R straight, then at each end of next R increase 1 st 1 time and 1 st every 6th R 7 times — 76 (84) sts. Work straight to 49 (51) cm or 19¼" (20").

Shape Neck and Shoulders: Cast off center 20 sts and work on each side separately. At neck edge, in every 2nd R cast off 2 sts 2 times and 1 st 1 time. *At the same time,* at armhole edge, in every 2nd R cast off 4 (5) sts 2 (3) times, 5 (6) sts 3 (2) times.

Left Front: Using finer needles and ecru cast on 30 (34) sts and work in K 1, P 1 rib for 4 cm or 1½". Change to thicker needles and work in st st and Color Sequence to Knitting Diagram. Set pattern R thus: K sts 3 (7)–8 1 time, repeat sts 1–8 3 (4) times. Continue in pattern, shaping side, armhole, and shoulder as for Back. *At the same time,* shape Front slope at 25 (27) cm or 10" (10½") by decreasing 1 st in next R then every 12th R 6 times.

Right Front: Work as for Left Front, reversing shapings and Knitting Diagram.

Finishing: Press lightly on wrong side. Join shoulder seams. Using finer needles, ecru, and with right side facing pick up and K 100 (104) sts along armhole edges and work 4 cm or 1½" in K 1, P 1 rib. Cast off in rib. Using circular needle and ecru, pick up and K 65 (68) sts along each straight front edge, 68 sts from front slopes, and 31 sts from back neck edge. Work back and forth in K 1, P 1 rib for 4 cm or 1½". Cast off in rib. Sew up side seams.

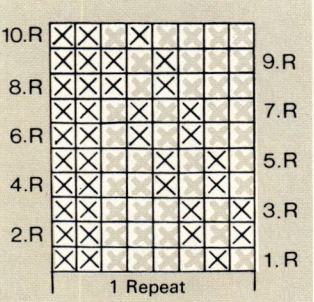

Knitting Diagram: 1 repeat of 8 sts is given.
Every cross = 1 stitch
Light brown cross = brown
Dark brown cross = ecru

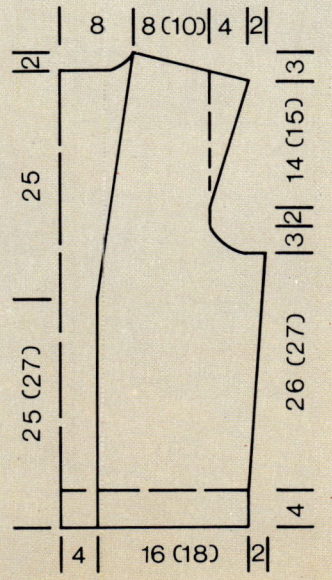

Half-pattern for small (large) size. The numbers are centimeters; inches are given in the directions.

Striking in black, white, and grey

Here is a sweater that is smart and dramatic. It combines plain bands with a tweed yarn decorated with a pattern of black diamonds.

Knitting

Size: Directions are for 88 cm or 34½" bust. Changes for 96 cm or 37½" bust are in brackets.

Materials Required:

300 (350) gm or 11 (13) oz black-and-white mixture, 50 gm or 2 oz each of black and white [100 gm = 360 m or 390 yds]. Knitting needles and circular needle size 4 (Am) or 9 (Eng). Stitch holder.

Basic Stitch: St st.

Tension: 25 sts and 36 R = 10 cm or 4".

Abbreviations: K = knit. P = purl. St(s) = stitch(es). St st = stocking or stockinette stitch. R = row(s). Rnd(s) = round(s).

DIRECTIONS

Back: Using black, cast on 119 (129) sts and work 3 R black, 14 R white, and 4 R black in K 1, P 1 rib. Break off black and white, join on mixed yarn and work in Basic Stitch for 8 R. Now working in mixed and black yarn, follow the pattern chart for 32 R.

Begin the 1st R with 12th–14th sts (14th st only), then work the repeat 8 (9) times, then 1st–4th (2nd) st. Continue thus, following chart until pattern is complete. Then work straight in st st in mixed yarn only for 5 cm or 2½", then decrease 1 st each end of every 12th R 5 times – 109 (119) sts. Work straight to 25 cm or 10", then increase 1 st each end of next R and again after 30 R – 113 (123) sts. Work straight to 45 cm or 17½".

Shape Armholes: At the beginning of every R, cast off 3 sts 2 times, 3 (4) sts 4 times, and 1 st 12 times – 83 (89) sts. Work straight to 62 (63) cm or 24½" (24¾").

Shape Neck and Shoulders: Cast off center 27 sts and work on each side separately. At neck edge, decrease 2 sts in every 2nd R 3 times then 1 st 2 times. *At the same time,* at 63 (64) cm or 24¾" (25¼") cast off 5 sts at beginning of next armhole edge R, then 5 (6) sts every 2nd R 3 times.

Front: Work to match Back to 40 (41) cm or 15½" (16").

Divide for Neck: Cast off center st and work on each side separately – 56 (61) sts each side. At neck edge, decrease 1 st every 2nd R 12 times, then 1 st every 4th R 6 times, and 1 st every 6th R 3 times. *At the same time,* at 45 cm or 17½", shape armhole to match Back and at 63 (64) cm or 24¾" (25¼") shape shoulder to match Back.

Sleeves: Using black, cast on 56 (62) sts and work cuff in rib as for Back border. Continue in mixed yarn, increasing 1 st each end of every 10th R 14 times – 84 (90) sts. Continue straight to 45 cm or 17½".

Shape Top: At beginning of every R cast off 4 sts 2 times, 2 sts 6 times, 1 st 28 (32) times, 2 sts 8 times, and 4 sts 2 times. Cast off remaining 12 (14) sts.

Neck Border: Using circular needle and black, cast on 210 sts and work in rnds of K 1, P 1 rib. Mark center K st and in every 2nd rnd work 3 sts together at V. Work 3 rnds black, 14 rnds white, and 3 rnds black. Cast off loosely in rib.

Finishing: Press work with a warm iron over damp cloth. Join all seams. Sew on Neck Border neatly.

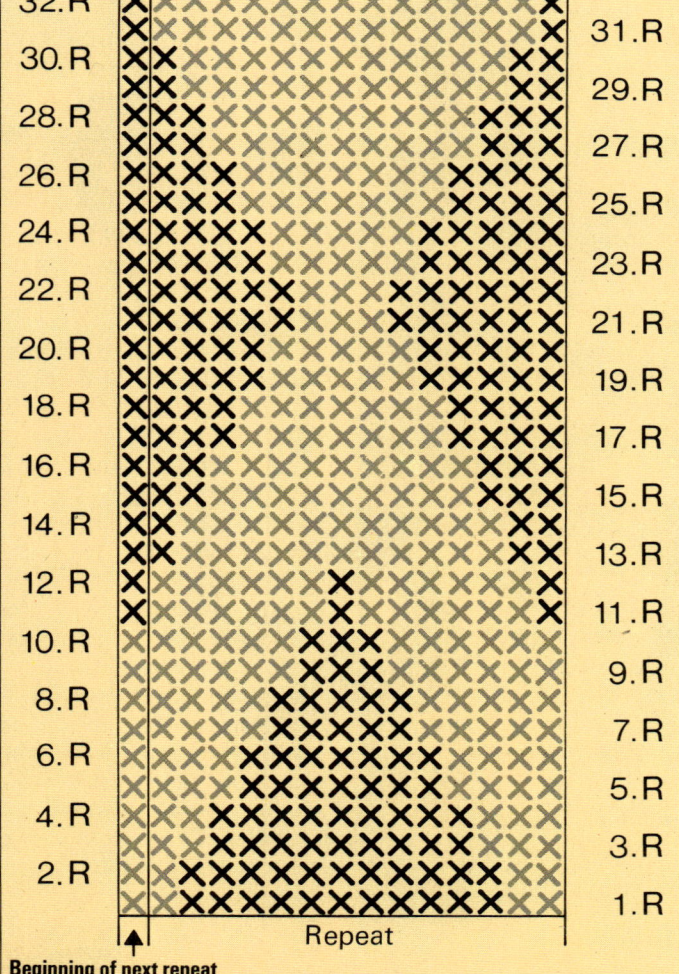

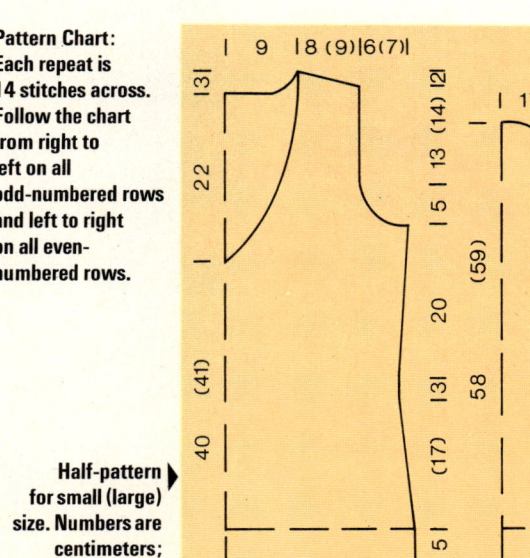

Pattern Chart: Each repeat is 14 stitches across. Follow the chart from right to left on all odd-numbered rows and left to right on all even-numbered rows.

Half-pattern for small (large) size. Numbers are centimeters; inches are in the directions.

1685

Mix-and-match at random

This is no ordinary twinset. The warm roll-neck pullover has its own toning sleeveless cardigan.

Size: Directions are for 88 cm or 34½″ bust. Changes for 96 cm or 37½″ bust are in brackets.

Materials Required:

Pullover: 400 (480) gm or 15 (17) oz blue/white mixture.
Cardigan: 120 (160) gm or 5 (6) oz blue/white mixture, 160 (200) gm or 6 (8) oz white [40 gm = 99 m or 108 yds]. Knitting needles sizes 2 and 4 (Am) or 10 and 11 (Eng). Circular needle size 2 (Am) or 11 (Eng). 6 buttons. St holder.

Basic Stitch: St st.
Color Sequence: (for Cardigan) *8 R blue/white, 4 R white, repeat from *.
Tension: 22 sts and 36 R = 10 cm or 4″.
Abbreviations: K = knit. P = purl. St(s) = stitch(es). R = row(s). Rnd(s) = round(s). St st = stocking or stockinette stitch.

PULLOVER

Back: Using blue/white mixture and finer needles,

cast on 102 (110) sts and work 8 cm or 3" in K 1, P 1 rib. Change to thicker needles and work in st st, decreasing 1 st each end of 1st R and every 10th R 3 times more — 94 (102) sts. Work straight for 5 R, then increase 1 st each end of next and every 20th R 3 times — 102 (110) sts. Work straight to 37 cm or $14\frac{1}{2}$".

Shape Armholes: At beginning of every R, cast off 3 (5) sts 2 times, 2 sts 6 times, 1 st 4 times, then 1 st each end of every 4th R 2 times — 76 (80) sts. Work straight to 56 (57) cm or 22" ($22\frac{1}{2}$").

Shape Neck and Shoulders: Cast off center 26 sts; work on each side separately. At neck edge, in every 2nd R cast off 2 sts 2 times and 1 st 1 time. *At the same time,* at armhole edge, in every 2nd R cast off 5 (5) sts 2 times and 5 (6) sts 2 times.

Front: Work as for Back to 49 (50) cm or $19\frac{1}{4}$" ($19\frac{1}{2}$").

Shape Neck: Cast off center 6 sts and work on each side separately. At neck edge, in every 2nd R cast off 3 sts 2 times, 2 sts 2 times, 1 st 2 times, then 1 st on every 4th R 3 times. *At the same time,* shape shoulder as for Back.

Sleeves: Using blue/white mixture and finer needles, cast on 48 (52) sts and work in K 1, P 1 rib for 8 cm or 3". Change to thicker needles and st st and increase across 1st R thus: K 4 (6), * increase in next st, K 2, repeat from * to last 2 (4) sts, K to end — 62 (66) sts. Continue in st st, increasing 1 st each end of every 18th (14th) R 7 (9) times — 76 (84) sts. Work straight to 46 cm or 18".

Shape Top: At beginning of every R, cast off 4 (6) sts 2 times, 3 sts 2 times, 2 sts 6 times, 1 st 4 times, then 1 st each end of every 4th R 4 times, then at beginning of every R, cast off 1 st 4 times, 2 sts 6 times, 3 sts 2 times, and 4 (5) sts 2 times. Cast off remaining 8 (12) sts.

Finishing: Pin out work and steam lightly. Join all seams. Using circular needle and blue/white mixture, pick up and K 110 sts around neck edge and work in rnds of K 1, P 1 rib for 24 cm or $9\frac{1}{2}$". Cast off in rib. Fold collar in half to right side.

CARDIGAN

Back: Using finer needles and white, cast on 106 (114) sts and work 8 cm or 3" in K 1, P 1 rib. Change to thicker needles and st st and work in Color Sequence to 36 cm or 14".

Shape Armholes: At beginning of every R, cast off 5 sts 2 times, 3 sts 2 times, 2 sts 4 times, 1 st 6 times, then 1 st each end of every 4th R 3 times — 70 (78) sts. Work straight to 56 (57) cm or 22" ($22\frac{1}{2}$").

Shape Neck: Cast off center 34 sts and work on each side separately. At neck edge, in every 2nd R cast off 2 sts 2 times and 1 st 3 times. *At the same time,* at 59 (60) cm or $23\frac{1}{4}$" ($23\frac{1}{2}$"), shape shoulder in every 2nd R at armhole edge by casting off 5 (7) sts 1 time and 6 (8) sts 1 time.

Left Front: Using white and finer needles, cast on 48 (52) sts and work in K 1, P 1 rib for 8 cm or 3". Change to thicker needles and st st and shape armhole as for Back, keeping front edge straight to 46 (47) cm or 18" ($18\frac{1}{2}$").

Shape Front: At neck edge, in every 2nd R cast off 4 sts 1 time, 3 sts 1 time, 2 sts 3 times, 1 st 2 times, then decrease 1 st every 4th R 4 times. Work straight at this edge and at 59 (60) cm or $23\frac{1}{4}$" ($23\frac{1}{2}$"), shape shoulder as for Back.

Right Front: Work to match Left Front, reversing all shapings.

Finishing: Pin out work and steam lightly. Join all seams. Using circular needle, white, and with right side facing, pick up and K 110 sts around each armhole edge and work in rnds of K 1, P 1 rib for 3 cm or $1\frac{1}{4}$". Cast off in rib. Using circular needle, white, and with right side facing, pick up and K 116 (118) sts along Front straight edges, 38 sts along each Front neck edge, and 51 sts from Back neck edge.

Working back and forth in K 1, P 1 rib, increase 1 st at neck edge in every 2nd R to 1.5 cm or $\frac{5}{8}$". Keeping increase at corner throughout, work buttonholes over 5 sts in next R, placing the first one 2 cm or $\frac{3}{4}$" from lower Right Front edge and 5 more at 6.5 cm or $2\frac{1}{2}$" intervals. In next R, cast on 5 sts in place of those cast off. Work to 3 cm or $1\frac{1}{4}$", then cast off in rib. Sew on the buttons.

The pullover and sleeveless cardigan look equally stylish worn separately. The basic stitch is stocking or stockinette stitch and the borders, cuffs, and roll-neck are ribbed.

Half-patterns for small (large) size for Cardigan (right) and Pullover (left, with sleeve center). Numbers are centimeters, inches are in the directions.

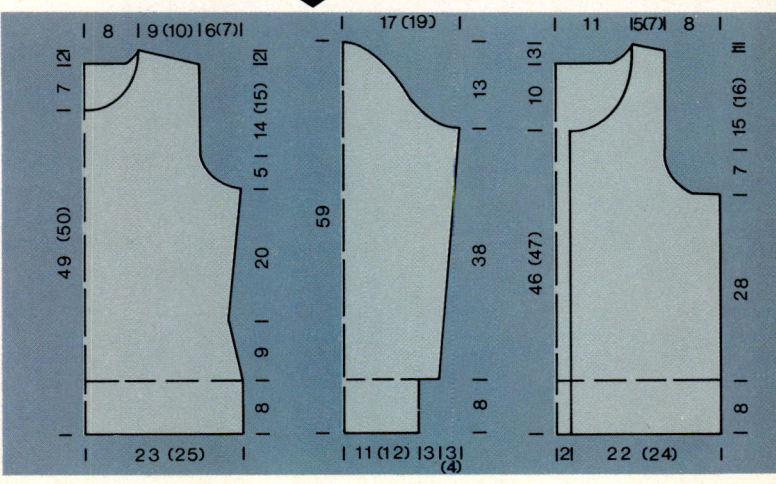

Sweet dreamer

The dirndl jackets are knitted in rib with garter stitch neck bands. The sleeves and hem have narrow contrasting borders and cords are drawn through at the neck and waist.

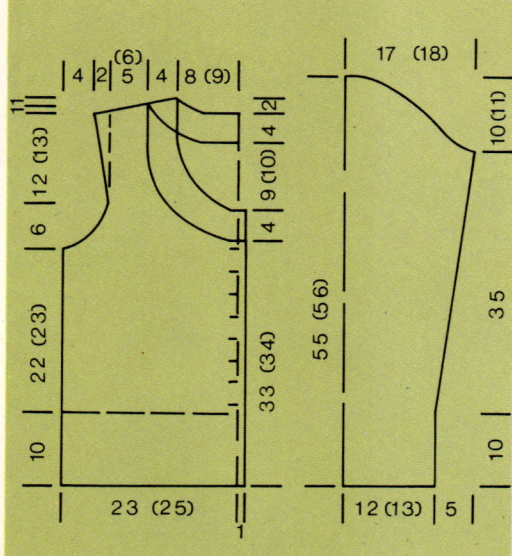

Half-pattern for small (large) size. The numbers are centimeters; inches are in the directions.

Size: Directions are for 88 cm or 34½" bust. Changes for 96 cm or 37½" bust are in brackets.

Materials Required:

450 (500) gm or 16 (18) oz black or white, 50 gm or 2 oz each red and green [50 gm = 150 m or 165 yds]. Knitting needles size 2 (Am) or 11 (Eng). 8 buttons.

Basic Stitch: K 1, P 1 rib.

Tension: 30 sts and 40 R (slightly stretched) = 10 cm or 4".

Abbreviations: K = knit. P = purl. St(s) = stitch(es). R = row(s).

DIRECTIONS

Back: Using green or red, cast on 137 (149) sts and work 1 R in K 1, P 1 rib. Change to black or white and continue in rib to 10 cm or 4". Work a R of holes thus: *rib 4, work 2 together, yarn over, repeat from *, ending rib 5. Continue in rib to 32 (33) cm or 12½" (13").

Shape Armholes: At beginning of every R, cast off 3 sts 4 times, 2 sts 6 times, and 1 st 12 times — 101 (113) sts. Work 4 R straight then increase 1 st each end of next R and every 8th R 5 times — 113 (125) sts.

Shape Neck and Shoulders: Cast off center 29 (35) sts and work on each side separately. At neck edge, in every 2nd R cast off 3 sts 3 times, 2 sts 5 times, and 1 st 2 times. *At the same time,* at 50 (52) cm or 19½" (20½") at armhole edge, in every 2nd R cast off 7 (8) sts 3 times.

Right Front: Using green or red, cast on 73 (79) sts and work 1 R in K 1, P 1 rib. Change to black or white. Work to 10 cm or 4", then work a R of holes as for Back, but end rib 1. Continue straight to 11 (12) cm or 4¼" (4¾"), ending at front edge. In next R, work buttonhole by casting off the 5–7th sts from edge, then in next R cast on 3 sts in place of those cast off. Make 7 more at 3 cm or 1¼" intervals.

Shape Armhole with decreases and increases as for Back, and work straight to 33 (34) cm or 13" (13½"), ending at front edge.

Shape Neck: Rib 10 and place on safety pin. At neck edge, in every 2nd R cast off 2 sts 7 (8) times, 1 st 13 (14) times, and 1 st every 4th R 3 times. Shape shoulder as for Back at 50 (52) cm or 19½" (20½").

Left Front: As for Right Front, reversing shaping and omitting buttonholes.

Sleeves: Using green or red, cast on 74 (80) sts and rib 1 R. Change to black or white and work in rib to 10 cm or 4". Increase 1 st each end of next R and on every 10th R 13 times — 102 (108) sts. Work to 45 cm or 17¾".

Shape Top: At beginning of every R, cast off 3 sts 4 (6) times. Cast off.

Finishing: Join seams. Using green or red and with right side facing, K across the 2 sets of 10 sts, pick up and K 176 (190) sts between them around front and back neck. Work in garter st with 4 R green or red, 12 R red or green, 4 R green or red. *At the same time,* mark 10th (9th) st from right edge and every 16th st, then on 3rd R and every 4th R 3 times, work marked st together with next st. *At the same time,* in the 6th R of the wide green or red band, work a R of holes over the 172 (184) sts thus: K 2, *K 2, K 2 together, yarn around needle, K 2, repeat from * to last 2 sts, K 2.

Make 2 twisted cords in red or green and thread through holes at the waist and at the neck border. Sew on the buttons.

Wear a dirndl jacket and let your imagination take you to flower-strewn Alpine meadows! This style looks charming with a gathered skirt.

Tyrolean touch

A pretty little girl in a bright dirndl jacket is an irresistible combination. The directions for this knitted jacket are given in two color variations and four sizes.

Sizes: Directions are for 56 cm or 22" chest. Changes for 61, 64, 66 cm or 24", 25", 26" chest are in brackets.

Materials Required:

150 (200:250:300) gm or 6 (8:9:11) oz white or red for main color, 50 gm or 2 oz each red, white, and green for contrasts. Knitting needles size 2 (Am) or 11 (Eng). Circular knitting needle size 1 (Am) or 12 (Eng). Crochet hook size B (Am) or 2.00 (Eng). 5 (6:6:7) buttons. St holders.

Basic Stitch: K 1, P 1 rib.
Tension: 36 sts and 33 R = 10 cm or 4".
Abbreviations: K = knit. P = purl. St(s) = stitch(es). R = row(s).

DIRECTIONS

Back: Using red or green, cast on 101 (107:113:119) sts and work in K 1, P 1 rib for 2 R. Continue in rib in white or red and work to 5 (5:6:6) cm or 2½" (2½":3":3"). Work a R of holes thus: *work 4 sts, yarn around needle, K 2 together, repeat from *, rib end sts. Work straight to 18 (21:23:26) cm or 7" (8¼":9":10¼").

Shape Armholes: At beginning of every R, cast off 3 sts 2 (2:4:4) times, 2 sts 6 (6:4:4) times, and 1 st 4 (4:6:6) times – 79 (85:87:93) sts. Work straight for 1 cm or $\frac{3}{8}$", then increase 1 st at each end of next R and every 6th (8th:8th:10th) R 3 times – 87 (93:95:101) sts. *At the same time,* at 25 (29:32:36) cm or 10" (11½":12½":14"), shape neck by placing center 35 (35:41:41) sts on st holder and working on each side separately. At neck edge, in every 2nd R cast off 3 sts 2 times, 2 sts 4 times, and 1 st 4 times.

At 30 (34:37:41) cm or 11¾" (13¼": 14½":16") – 8 (11:9:12) sts, cast off.

Right Front: Using red or green, cast on 54 (58:62:66) sts and work as for Back to 6 (6:8:8) cm or 2½" (2½":3":3"). In next R, work buttonhole by casting off the 5th-7th sts from front edge. In following R, cast on 3 sts in place of those cast off. Work 4 (5:5:6) more buttonholes at 3 cm or 1¼" intervals without further instructions and work armhole decreases and increases to match Back until work measures 19 (22:25: 28) cm or 7½" (8½":10":11"), ending at front edge.

Shape Neck: Keeping continuity of armhole increases, slip first 8 (8:10: 10) sts on st holder, then at neck edge, in every 2nd R cast off 4 sts 1 time, 3 sts 3 times, 2 sts 5 (5:6:6) times, and 1 st 8 (9:9:10) times. When work measures same as Back to shoulder, cast off the 8 (11:9:12) sts.

Left Front: Work to match Right Front, reversing all shapings and omitting buttonholes.

Sleeves: Using red or green, cast on 60 (64:66:70) sts and work 2 R in Basic Stitch, then work 12 R green or red, and 3 R red or green. Change to white or red and work for 5 cm or 2", then increase 1 st each end of next R and every 8th R 9 (10:13:14) times – 80 (86:94:100) sts. Work straight to 27 (30:33:36) cm or 10½" (11¾":13":14").

Shape Top: At beginning of every R, cast off 3 sts 8 (6:4:2) times, 2 sts 12 (20:28:34) times, and 3 sts 6 (4:2:2) times. Cast off remaining 14 (16:20:20) sts.

Yoke: Join small shoulder seams. Using circular needle and green or white, begin at Right Front edge and K across the 8 (8:10:10) sts, working together the 4th and 5th sts and 9th and 10th sts – 7 (7:8:8) sts on needle. Pick up and K 58 (60:60:62) sts to sts on Back st holder. K across Back sts, working together the 4th and 5th and 9th and 10th sts from each end. Pick up and K 58 (60:60: 62) sts to Left Front st holder, K across sts on holder as for Right Front – 161 (165:173:177) sts.

Now work back and forth in garter st in color sequence of 1 R green or white, 2 R red or green, 14 R green or red, 2 R red or green, 8 R white, 1 R red or green, cast off in last color used. *At the same time,* decrease 14 sts evenly in every 6th R 4 times. 1st decrease will be: K 7 (11:5:9), * K2 together, K 9 (9:10:10), repeat from * 13 times more. Also, in the 5th R of white stripe work a R of holes as at waist.

Finishing: Join remaining seams. Work 1 R of slip stitch in red or green up each front edge, then work 1 R of single crochet (Am) or double crochet (Eng). Fasten off.

Embroidery: In the center of the green or red yoke stripe, work a small cross at 3 cm or 1⅛" intervals, using red or green. Work 6 lazy daisy petals in white around these crosses.

Make cords in red or green and draw through holes at waist and neck. Sew on buttons.

Simple, white lazy daisy stitch flowers deck the garter stitch yoke, and contrasting cords draw in the neck and waist.

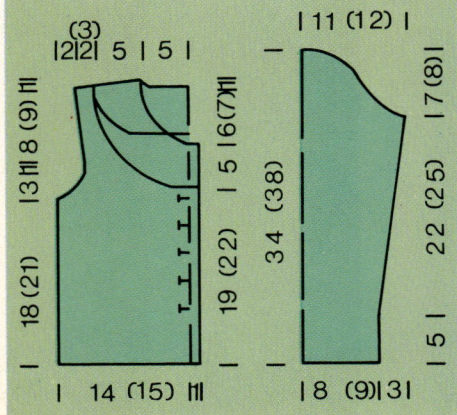

Half-pattern for the two smallest sizes. The numbers are centimeters; inches are given in the directions.

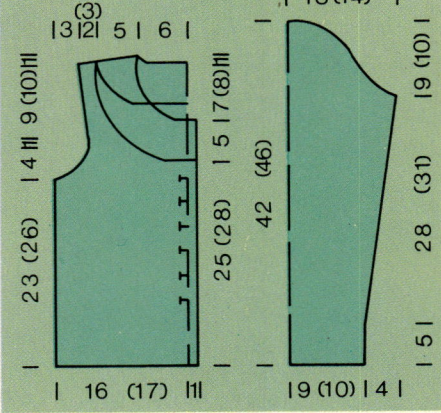

Half-pattern for the two largest sizes. The numbers are centimeters; inches are given in the directions.

Knitted tank tops with child appeal!
Two's company

Size: Directions are for 56 cm or 22" chest. Changes for 59 (64:66) cm or 23" (25":26") chest are in brackets.

Materials Required:

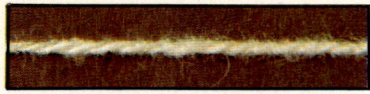

150 (150:200:200) gm or 6 (6:8:8) oz white [100 gm = 247 m or 270 yds]. Yarn for embroidery. Knitting needles sizes 2 and 4 (Am) or 9 and 11 (Eng). Circular needle size 2 (Am) or 11 (Eng). Cable needle.

Basic Pattern: See Knitting Diagram which shows the right half of back or front plus 1 center st. Follow diagram from right to center st, then work in reverse to 1st st for other half. Work all sts on wrong side R as they present themselves. Repeat R 3–26 throughout. To cross 1 + 2 sts to right, place 1 st onto cable needle behind the work, K2 sts, then P st on cable needle. To cross 2 + 1 sts to left, place 2 sts onto cable needle in front of work, P next st, then K sts on cable needle.

Tension: 27 sts and 36 R = 10 cm or 4".

Abbreviations: K = knit. P = purl. St(s) = stitch(es). R = row(s). Rnd(s) = round(s).

DIRECTIONS

Back: Using finer needles and white, cast on 83 (87:93:97) sts and work in K 1, P 1 rib for 6 (6:6:7) cm or 2½" (2½":2½": 2¾"). Change to thicker needles and work in Basic Pattern with Knitting Diagram. For 1st size: K 1 (edge st), then work 1st–40th sts, slip center st purlwise, then work in reverse from 40th –1st sts, K edge st. For 2nd size: Work as for 1st size, but after first slip st (16th st from beginning), P 1 extra st, then P 1 extra st before next slip st. Work to match other half. For 3rd size: Work as for 1st size, but P 1 extra st before and after each slip st. For 4th size: Work as for 3rd size, but P 1 st after first edge st and P 1 st before last edge st.

Work in pattern as set to 20 (23:25:29) cm or 8" (9":10": 11½").

Shape Armholes: At beginning of every R, cast off 4 (4:5:7) sts 2 times, 3 sts 4 times, 2 sts 4 times, and 1 st 2 times — 53 (57:61:61) sts. Work straight to 31 (34:37:41) cm or 12¼" (13¼":14½":16").

Shape Neck: Cast off center 19 (19:23:23) sts and work on each side separately. At neck edge, in every 2nd R cast off 2 sts 2 times and 1 st 1 time. *At the same time,* at 32 (35:38: 42) cm or 12½" (13¾":14¼": 16½"), shape shoulder at armhole edge in every 2nd R by casting off 6 (7:7:7) sts 2 times.

Front: Work as for Back to 18 (21:21:25) cm or 7" (8¼": 8¼":9¾"). Continue to shape armhole and shoulder as for Back, but shape neck thus: slip center st onto safety pin and work on each side of center separately. At neck edge, decrease 1 st in every 2nd R 8 times, 1 st at beginning of every 4th R 4 times, and 1 st at beginning of every 6th R 2 (2: 4:4) times.

Finishing: Join shoulders. With circular needle pick up and K 116 (116:136:136) sts around neck, including st left on safety pin. Work in K 1, P 1 rib for 3 cm or 1¼" and at center front in every rnd, slip 2, K 1, pass slipped sts over. Cast off in rib.

Pick up and K 80 (80:86:86) sts around each armhole and work in rnds of K 1, P 1 rib for 3 cm or 1¼". Cast off in rib. Embroider the fronts as shown in photographs. For the boy's pullover, thread yarn through sts to form vertical lines.

The zigzag pattern is embroidered with crosses secured with running stitch.

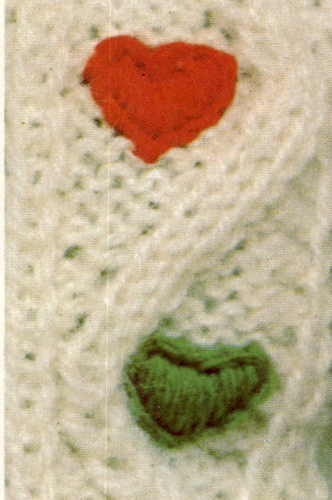

The hearts are embroidered in satin stitch and outlined in stem stitch.

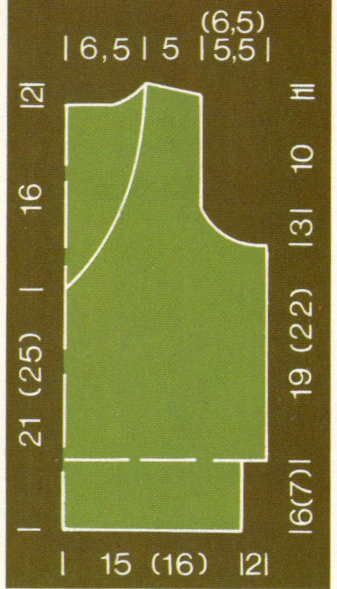

Half-pattern for 3rd (4th) size. Numbers are centimeters; see inches in directions.

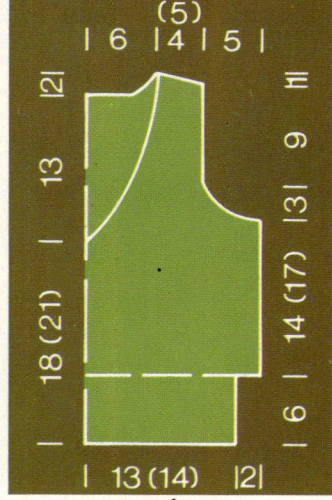

Knitting Diagram shows the right half of back or front plus center stitch. Follow diagram from 1st st to center and back for each right side row. Work stitches on wrong side as they appear.

Half-pattern for 1st (2nd) size. Numbers are centimeters; see inches in directions.

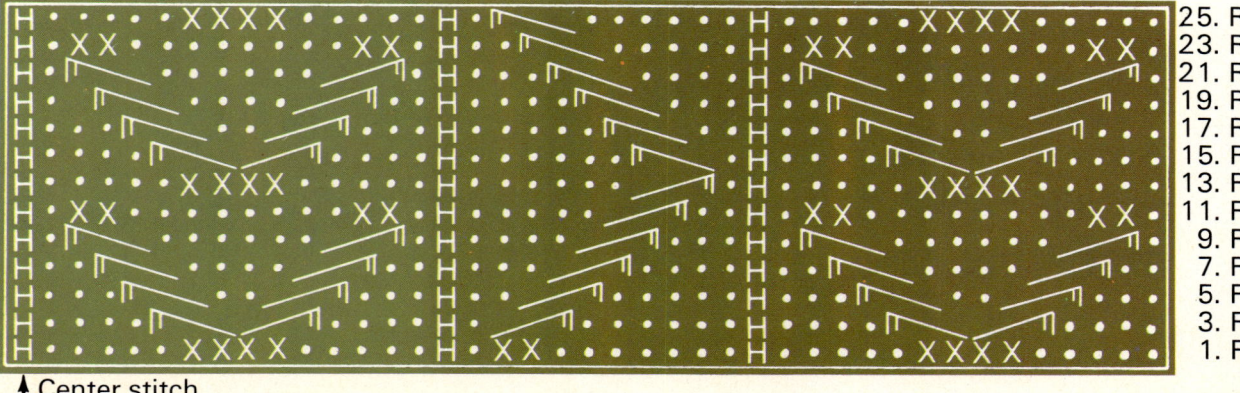

= Knit
= Purl
= Slip 1 st purlwise on right side R; purl on wrong side R
= Cross 1 + 2 stitches to the right
= Cross 2 + 1 stitches to the left

↑ Center stitch

Openwork pattern

 How-to

1 R 1: (right side in 1st color) K 1 (edge st), K 6, *slip 2 purlwise with yarn behind the piece, K 6, repeat from *, ending K 1 (edge st). R 2: K 1, P 6, *slip 2 purlwise with yarn in front of the piece, P 6, repeat from *, ending K 1.

2 R 3: K 5, *slip next 2 sts onto cable needle at back, K 1st slipped st. . . .

3 . . . K together the 2 sts from cable needle, bring yarn forward to make a st, and slip the 2nd slipped st onto cable needle at front of work. K the next 2 sts together, then K st from cable needle, K 2. Repeat from * to last 3 sts, K 3.

4 R 4: P, working P 1, K 1 into each "made" st. R 5: Change color, K 3, continue from * of R 1 to last 5 sts, slip 2 purlwise, K 3. R 6: K 1, P 2, work from * of R 2 to last 5 sts, slip 2 purlwise, P 2, K 1. R 7: K 1, work from * of R 3, ending last repeat K 1 instead of K 2. R 8: Repeat R 4. Repeat R 1–8.

Size: Directions are for 62 cm or 24½" chest. Changes for 69 cm or 27" chest are in brackets.

Materials Required:

150gm or 6oz beige, 100 gm or 4oz blue [50gm = 160m or 176yds]. Knitting needles sizes 2 and 4 (Am) or 9 and 11 (Eng). Circular needle size 2 (Am) or 11 (Eng). 5 buttons. Cable needle.

Basic Pattern: See How-to.
Color Sequence: 4 R alternately blue and beige.
Tension: 28 sts and 42 R = 10 cm or 4".
Abbreviations: K = knit. P = purl. St(s) = stitch(es). R = row(s).

DIRECTIONS

Back: Using finer needles and beige, cast on 80 (88) sts and work in K 1, P 1 rib, working 15 R beige, 2 R blue, and 3 R beige. ** In next R, using beige, increase thus: * rib 4 (5), increase in next st, rib 5 (5), repeat from * 7 times more — 88 (96) sts. Change to thicker needles and work in Basic Pattern and Color Sequence to 24 (26) cm or 9½" (10¼").

Shape Armholes: At beginning of every R, cast off 4 sts 2 times, 2 sts 4 times, 1 st 8 times — 64 (72) sts. Work straight to 36 (40) cm or 14" (15¾").

Shape Neck and Shoulders: Cast off center 22 sts and work on each side separately. At neck edge, in every 2nd R cast off 2 sts 2 times and 1 st 1 time. *At the same time,* at 37 (41) cm or 14½" (16") at armhole edge, in every 2nd R cast off 5 (6) sts 1 time, 5 (7) sts 1 time, and 6 (7) sts 1 time.

Left Front: Using finer needles and beige, cast on 36 (44) sts and work rib as for Back to **. In next R, increase across R thus: rib 4, * increase in next st, rib

Party best

The unusual two-tone pattern makes this a very special cardigan for pretty little girls.

7 (9), repeat from * 3 times more — 40 (48) sts. Now shape armhole and shoulder as for Back and keep front edge straight to 32 (36) cm or 12½" (14"), ending at front edge.

Shape Neck: At beginning of next R, cast off 3 (4) sts, then in every 2nd R cast off 2 (3) sts 2 times and 1 st 5 (6) times.

Right Front: Work as for Left Front, reversing shapings and pattern placement.

Sleeves: Using finer needles and beige, cast on 46 (54) sts and work cuff as for Back rib to **. Increase in next R thus: For size 1, rib 5, increase in next 18 sts, rib 5; for size 2, increase in every 3rd st — 64 (72) sts. Change to thicker needles and Basic Pattern and work straight to 32 (35) cm or 12½" (13¾").

Shape Top: Keeping continuity of pattern, at beginning of every R cast off 3 sts 2 times, 2 sts 2 times, 1 st 34 (38) times, 2 sts 2 times, 3 sts 2 times. Cast off remaining 10 (14) sts.

Front Band: Using circular needle and beige, cast on 86 (96) sts for each front edge 77 sts for neck — 249 (269) sts in all. Mark the corner st on each side of neck sts. Work back and forth in K 1, P 1 rib, working 1 R beige, 2 R blue, and remainder in beige. *At the same time,* in every 2nd R increase each side of knitted marked st by picking up thread either side of st and knitting into back of it. Work to 1.5 cm or ½", ending at lower edge of Right Front. In next R, cast off 3 sts for buttonholes, placing 1st one 2.5 cm or 1" from lower edge and 4 more at 6 (7) cm or 2½" (2¾") intervals. In next R, cast on 3 sts in place of those cast off. Continue in rib to 3 cm or 1¼", increasing at corners as before. Cast off in rib.

Finishing: Join seams.

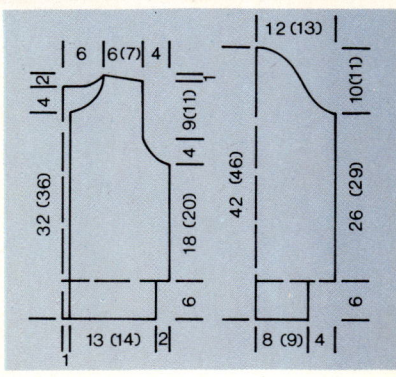

Half-pattern for the front, back, and sleeve in small (large) size. The numbers are centimeters; inches are given in the directions.

Sew on Band. Sew on buttons.

1695

FOR BOTH STYLES

Size: Directions are for 56 cm or 22" chest. Changes for 60 cm or 23¾" chest are in brackets.

Materials Required:

Colors and quantities are given in individual directions [40 gm = 69 m or 75 yds]. Knitting needles size 5 (Am) or 8 (Eng). 3 buttons. St holders.

Tension: (For Openwork Pattern) 18 sts and 33 R = 10 cm or 4".

Abbreviations: K = knit. P = purl. St(s) = stitch(es). St st = stocking or stockinette st. R = row(s).

GREEN PULLOVER

Yarn: 100 gm or 4 oz each in white and green/white mixture.

Openwork Pattern: R 1: (right side) White; K 1, *K 2 together, yarn around needle, repeat from * to last st, K 1. R 2: White; P all sts and "made" sts. R 3: Mixture; K. R 4: Mixture; K. R 5: Mixture; P. R 6: Mixture; K. Repeat R 1–6.

DIRECTIONS

Back, Front, Sleeves: Begin at neck edge. Using mixture, cast on 56 sts and work 2 cm or ¾" in K 1, P 1 rib.

Raglan Shaping: With yarn remnant in a different color, mark the 9th, 20th, 37th, and 48th st as a guide. Work in Openwork Pattern, but increase 1 st each side of marked sts on every right side R 14 (16) times — 168 (184) sts.

Divide for Back, Front, and Sleeves: Leave the 23 (25) sts of each Back half and 46 (50) sts of Front on st holders. Work the 38 (42) sts of each sleeve separately. Keeping continuity of pattern, cast on 2 sts at beginning of next 2 R and work on these 42 (46) sts, decreasing 1 st each end of every 4th R 5 times. *At the same time,* at 3 cm or 1¼" from division, cut white and continue in mixture in K 1, P 1 rib for 4 cm or 1½". Cast off in rib. Pick up Front 46 (50) sts and work in white only in st st, casting on 2 sts at beginning of first 2 R. Work straight to 17 (20) cm or 6¾" (8") from division. Change to mixture and work 4 cm or 1½" in K 1, P 1 rib. Cast off in rib. Join white to the 23 (25) sts of one Back half. Cast on 2 sts at armhole edge on next R and work as for Front. Repeat for other half.

Finishing: Pin out parts, cover with a damp cloth, and leave to dry. Join seams. Sew buttons down left Back half, and make 3 chain-stitch button-loops to correspond with buttons.

RED PULLOVER

Yarn: 150 gm or 6 oz each of white and red/white mixture.

Openwork Pattern: R 1: (right side) White; K. R 2: White; P. R 3: White, K 1, *K 2 together, yarn around needle, K 1, repeat from *, ending K 1. R 4: White; P. R 5–8: Mixture; Work R 3–6 of Green Pullover. Repeat R 1–8.

DIRECTIONS

Using mixture, cast on 56 sts and work 2 cm or ¾" in K 1, P 1 rib. Continue in Openwork Pattern, working Raglan Shaping as for Green Pullover. After the division and increases, work the Sleeves, keeping continuity of pattern over the 42 (46) sts, and decreasing 1 st each end in every 10th R 7 times — 28 (32) sts. Work straight to 26 (28) cm or 10¼" (11") from division, change to mixture, and work 4 cm or 1½" in K 1, P 1 rib. Cast off in rib. Work Front and Back in Openwork Pattern, following Green Pullover for shapings and measurements.

Finishing: See Green Pullover.

It's no secret

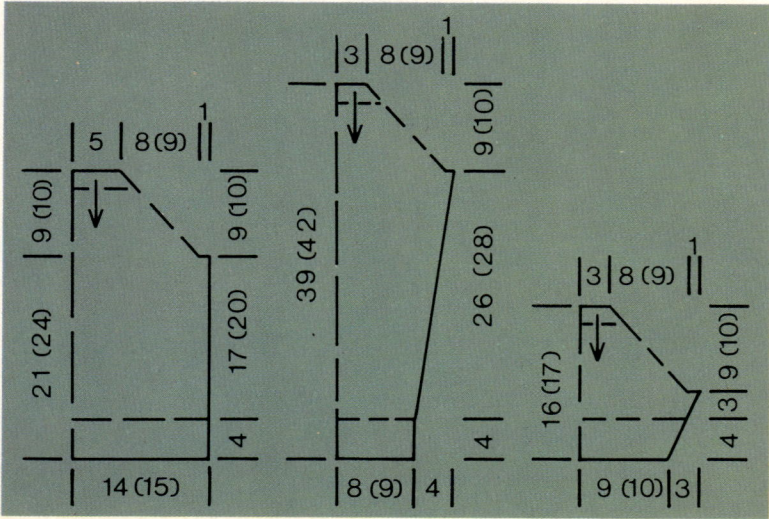

Half-pattern in small (large) size for Front and Back on the left, long sleeve in the center, and short sleeve on the right. The numbers are centimeters; inches are given in the directions. Arrows indicate the direction to work.

These pretty pullovers are made in cotton yarn. One has long sleeves and is patterned throughout, the other has short sleeves and a plain white bodice.

Candystripe kids

You can't beat stripes for cheerful sporty pullovers that the children will love. The pullovers are given in three sizes.

Size: Directions are for 58 cm or 23" chest. Changes for 62 cm and 66 cm or 24" and 26" chest are in brackets.

Materials Required:

100 (150:150) gm or 4 (6:6) oz red, green, or blue; 50 (100:100) gm or 2 (4:4) oz white [50 gm = 210 m or 230 yds]. Knitting needles sizes 1 and 2 (Am) or sizes 11 and 12 (Eng). Set of double-pointed needles size 1 (Am) or 12 (Eng).

Basic Stitch: St st.
Color Sequence: Alternately 4 R white and 4 R main color.

Tension: 26 sts and 38 R = 10 cm or 4".
Abbreviations: K = knit. P = purl. St(s) = stitch(es). St st = stocking or stockinette stitch. R = row(s). Rnd(s) = round(s).

DIRECTIONS

Back: Using finer needles and main color, cast on 78 (83:88) sts and work 5 cm or 2" in K 1, P 1 rib. Change to thicker needles and st st and work in Color Sequence to 20 (22:24) cm or 8" (8¾":9½") or length required.
Shape Armholes: At beginning of every R, cast off 3 sts 2 times, 2 sts 2 times, and 1 st 6 times — 62 (67:72) sts. Work straight to 32 (35:38) cm or 12½" (13¾":15").
Shape Neck and Shoulders: Cast off center 22 (23:22) sts and work on each side separately. At neck edge, in every 2nd R cast off 2 sts 2 times and 1 st 1 time. *At the same time,* at 33 (36:39) cm or 13" (14¼": 15½") at armhole edge, in every 2nd R cast off 7 (8: 10) sts 1 time and 8 (9:10) sts 1 time.
Front: Work as for Back to 27 (30:32) cm or 10½" (11¾":12½").
Shape Neck: Cast off center 8 (9:8) sts and work on each side separately. At neck edge, in every 2nd R cast off 3 sts 1 time, 2 sts 2 times, and 1 st 3 times, then 1 st every 4th R 2 times. *At the same time,* when work measures same as Back to shoulder, shape shoulder as for Back.
Sleeves: Using finer needles and main color, cast on 42 (42:46) sts and work 5 cm or 2" in K 1, P 1 rib. Change to thicker needles and continue in st st and Color Sequence, increasing 1 st each end of every 10th (12th:14th) and 12th (14th:16th) R alternately 8 times — 58 (58:62) sts. Work straight to 30 (33:36) cm or 11¾" (13":14¼") or length required.
Shape Top: At beginning of every R, cast off 3 sts 2 times, 2 sts 6 (4:6) times, 1 st 16 (20:20) times, 2 sts 6 times, and 3 sts 2 times. Cast off remaining 6 sts.
Finishing: Pin out and press work lightly on wrong side. Join shoulder seams. Using the double-pointed needles and with right side facing, pick up and K 112 (112:118) sts all around neck edge and work in rnds of K 1, P 1 rib for 2 cm or ¾". Cast off in rib. Join all seams. Press seams.

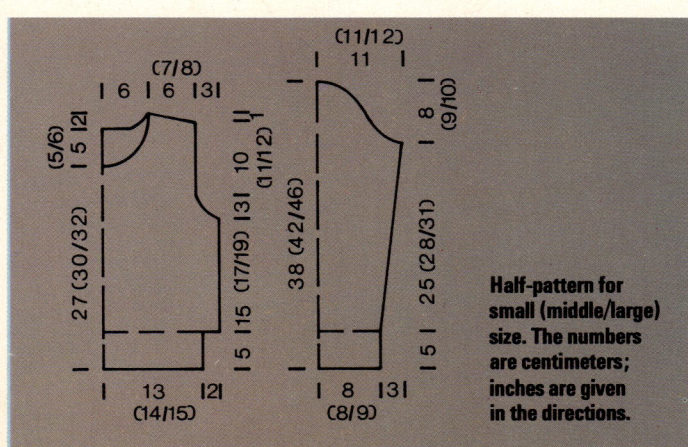

Half-pattern for small (middle/large) size. The numbers are centimeters; inches are given in the directions.

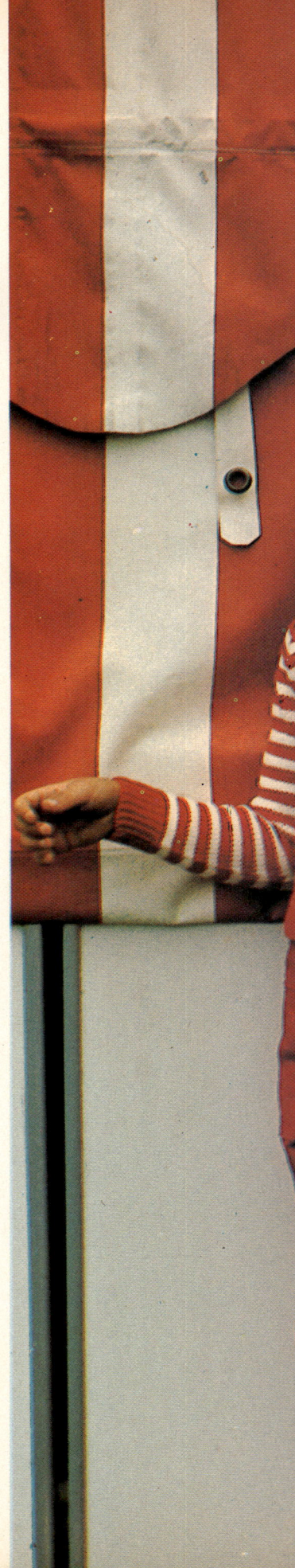

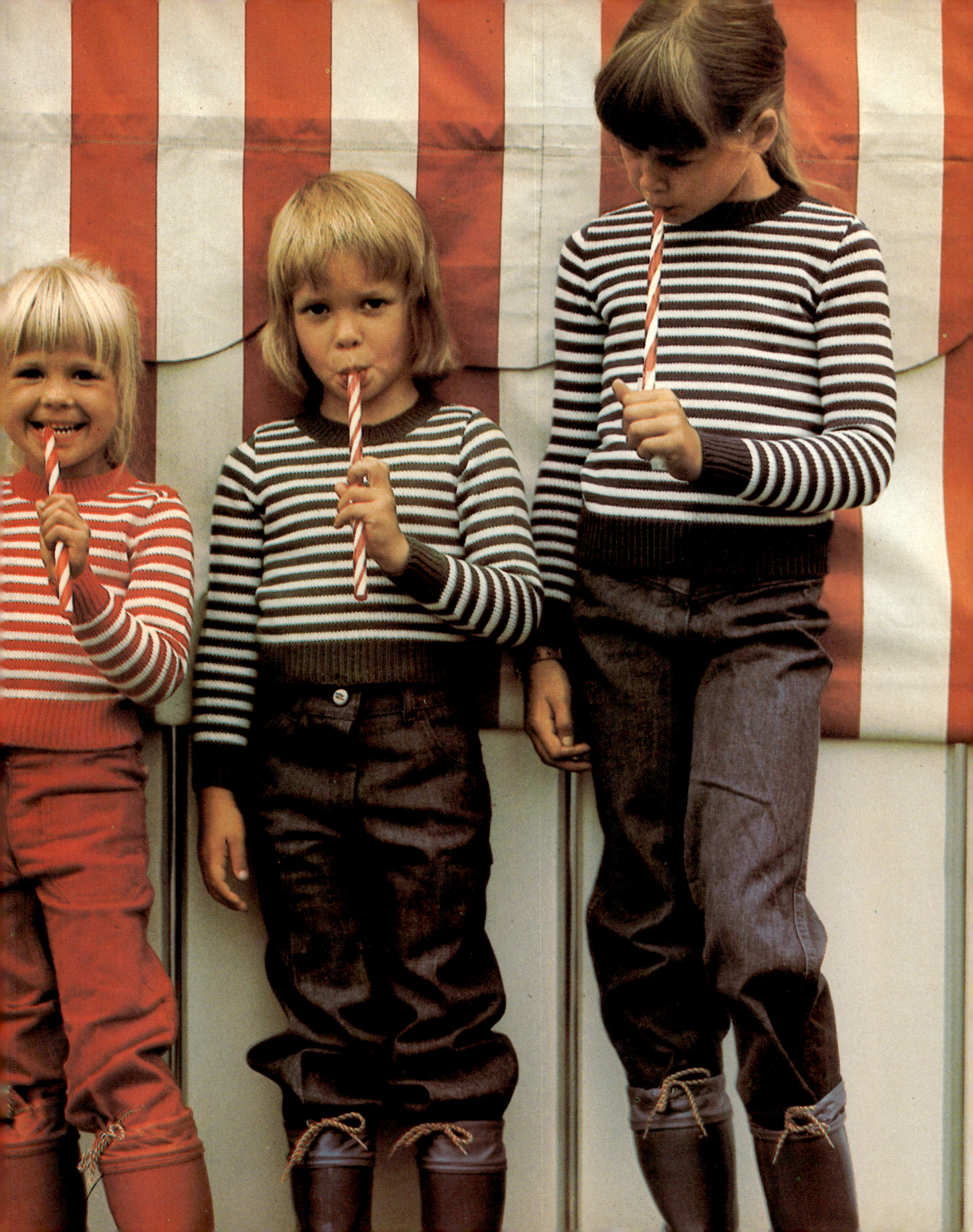

Treat your little girl to a super new dress. It's worked in rounds from top to bottom so that it can easily be lengthened.

Sugar and spice and all things nice

Size: To fit a 3–5 year old, height 98–110 cm or 38½"–43".

Materials Required:

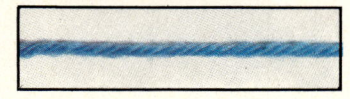

150 gm or 6 oz red, 50 gm or 2 oz white [50 gm = 137 m or 149 yds]. Circular needles sizes 1 and 2 (Am) or 11 and 12 (Eng). Knitting needles size 1 (Am) or 12 (Eng). St holders.

Basic Stitch: St st in rnds.

Color Sequence: Alternately 4 rnds white, 4 rnds red.

Tension: 26 sts and 38 rnds = 10 cm or 4".

Abbreviations: K = knit. P = purl. St(s) = stitch(es). R = row(s). Rnd(s) = round(s).

DIRECTIONS

Back and Front: Begin at neck edge and work Back and Front in one piece. Using red and finer circular needle, cast on 96 sts and work in rnds of K 1, P 1 rib. With colored thread, mark the 1st, 33rd, 49th, and 81st st for raglan seam. On each side of these sts, increase 1 st every 2nd R 23 times, always knitting the "marked" st and keeping continuity of rib sts between the 4 knitted sts.

When increases are complete, divide the 280 sts. Keep the 2 sets of 77 sts for Back and Front on st holders, and work on the sets of 63 sts separately for the sleeves. Change to the knitting needles and continue in rib in R, decreasing 1 st each end of every 2nd R 3 times — 57 sts. Work straight for 2 cm or ¾" and cast off in rib.

Transfer the 154 sts of Back and Front onto the thicker circular needle and work in rnds and Color Sequence, knitting together every 14th and 15th st in Rnd 1 — 144 sts. Now mark side seams (72 sts each on Back and Front). Increase 1 st at side seams every 4th rnd 26 times by picking up loop and knitting into back of it — 196 sts. K to 29 cm or 11½", then work 14 rnds of 1 rnd P, 1 rnd K to form garter st. Cast off.

Finishing: Join sleeve seams. Press st st parts with a warm iron over damp cloth. Turn up hem and stitch.

To Lengthen: When dress is too short and needs to be lengthened, work thus: remove the 14 rnds of border, then work 2 rnds each in white, blue, and red in garter st as before to required length. Cast off. To lengthen sleeve, remove cast-off edge and seam, and using knitting needles, work as for lower border of Back and Front in Color Sequence to required length, working in garter st. Cast off and sew up seam.

Half-pattern for small (large) size. Numbers are centimeters; inches are in the directions. Arrows show direction to work.

It's a piece of cake

Here are two scrumptious outfits to make a little girl feel pretty. One has a buttoned cardigan, the other a zipper fastened pullover, and both have matching skirts.

FOR BOTH
Size: Directions are for 62 cm or 24" chest. Changes for 66 cm or 26" chest are in brackets.
Materials Required:

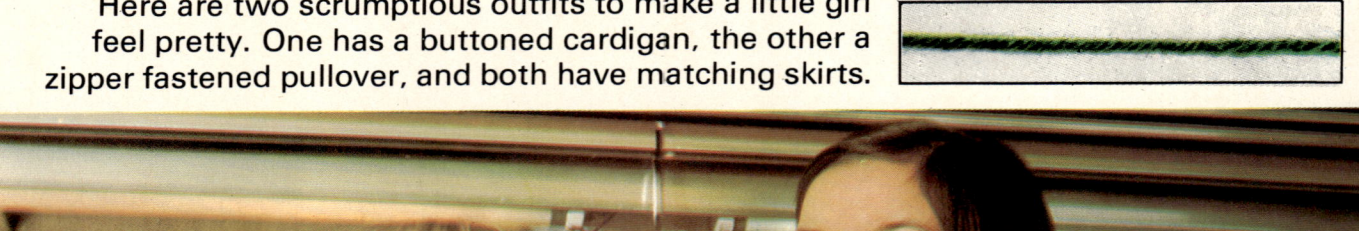

Style 1

Style 2

Quantities are given in individual directions [50 gm = 190 m or 209 yds]. Knitting needles and circular needles sizes 1 and 2 (Am) or 11 and 12 (Eng). 6 buttons. Waist elastic.

Basic Stitch: St st in R and K in rnds.

Color Sequence 1: *4 R or rnds blue, 2 white, 4 pink, 2 white, 4 green, 2 white, 4 yellow, 2 white, 4 lilac, 2 white, repeat from *.

Color Sequence 2: *2 R pink, 10 R white, 2 R blue, 10 R white, 2 R lilac, 10 R white, 2 R yellow, 10 R white, 2 R green, 10 R white, repeat from *.

Color Sequence 3: *4 R pink, 2 R white, 4 R blue, 2 R white, 4 R lilac, 2 R white, 4 R yellow, 2 R white, 4 R green, 2 R white, repeat from *.

Color Sequence 4: *2 R blue, 4 R white, 2 R pink, 4 R white, 2 R green, 4 R white, 2 R yellow, 4 R white, 2 R lilac, 4 R white, repeat from *.

Tension: 29 sts, 40 R = 10 cm or 4".

Abbreviations: K = knit. P = purl. St(s) = stitch(es). St st = stocking or stockinette stitch. R = row(s). Rnd(s) = round(s).

STYLE 1

Yarn: 150 gm or 6 oz white, 50 gm or 2 oz each of yellow, green, lilac, blue, and pink.

SKIRT

Using finer circular needle and white, begin at waist edge and cast on 176 (192) sts and work 2 cm or ¾" in K 1, P 1 rib. Now mark every 22nd (24th) st. Change to thicker circular needle and K in rnds and Color Sequence 1. In Rnd 1, pick up thread before marked st and K into back of thread — 184 (200) sts. Increase thus on every 6th rnd 14 (17) times, but alternate the increase by working next increase after marked st, and the following one before marked st — 296 (336) sts. Work straight to about 23 (28) cm or 9" (11"), ending after a complete color stripe of 4 R. Garter stitch border: Change to finer circular needle and white and work 1 rnd K, 1 rnd P. Repeat these 2 rnds, but now work 6 rnds instead of 4 in colors, keeping 2 rnds in white between colors. Work until 1 complete repeat of colors have been worked from last st st stripe. Cast off on last white rnd.

Finishing: Press. Work herringbone st st casing at waist. Insert elastic.

CARDIGAN

Back: Using finer needles and white, cast on 92 (98) sts and work 5 cm or 2" in K 1, P 1 rib. Change to thicker needles and work in st st, following Color Sequence 2 to 20 (23) cm or 8" (9").

Shape Armholes: At beginning of every R, cast off 3 sts 2 times, 2 sts 4 times, and 1 st 8 times — 70 (76) sts. Work straight to 34 (38) cm or 13½" (15").

Shape Neck and Shoulders: Cast off center 22 (28) sts and work on each side separately. At neck edge, in every 2nd R cast off 2 sts 1 time and 1 st 1 time. *At the same time,* at armhole edge, in every 2nd R cast off 7 sts 3 times.

Left Front: Using finer needles and white, cast on 42 (45) sts and work 5 cm or 2" in K 1, P 1 rib. Change to thicker needles and continue in st st and Color Sequence 2, shaping armhole and shoulder as for Back. *At the same time,* work straight at front edge to 29 (33) cm or 11½" (13"), then shape neck in every 2nd R by casting off 2 sts 3 (4) times and 1 st 4 (5) times.

Right Front: Work as for Left Front, reversing all shapings.

Sleeves: Using finer needles and white, cast on 60 (66) sts and work 3 cm or 1¼" in K 1, P 1 rib. Change to thicker needles and continue in st st and Color Sequence 3, increasing 1 st each end of every 2nd R 5 times — 70 (76) sts. Work to 6 cm or 2½".

Shape Top: At beginning of every R, cast off 3 sts 2 times, 2 sts 6 times, 1 st 20 (24) times, 2 sts 6 times, 3 sts 2 times — 14 (16) sts. Cast off.

Finishing: Press work. Join all seams. With right side of work facing and using finer needles and white, pick up and K 81 (91) sts around neck edge and work 3 cm or 1¼" in K 1, P 1 rib. Cast off in rib.

Using finer needles and white, begin at neck edge of Left Front, pick up and K 97 (109) sts down to lower edge. Work in K 1, P 1 rib for 3 cm or 1¼". Cast off in rib. Work other band to match, but begin at lower edge of Right Front and work 6 buttonholes. At 1.5 cm or ⅝", cast off 3 sts 2 (2.5) cm or ¾" (1") in from lower edge. Make 5 more 4.5 (5) cm or 1¾" (2") apart. In next R cast on 3 sts in place of these cast off. Sew on buttons.

STYLE 2

Yarn: 200 gm or 8 oz white, 50 gm or 2 oz each pink, blue, lilac, yellow, and green. Zipper: 15 cm (6") long.

SKIRT

Work as for other skirt, but after waistband work in Color Sequence 4 to garter st border, then continue as for Style 1.

PULLOVER

Back: Work as for Cardigan to 24 (28) cm or 9½" (11"), but after rib in white, work 1 complete st st set of stripes in color as for lower edge of skirt, then continue in white only.

Divide for Opening: Divide work at center and work straight on each side separately to 34 (38) cm or 13½" (15"), ending at armhole edge.

Shape Shoulder: At armhole edge, in every 2nd R cast off 7 sts 3 times. Cast off remaining 14 (17) sts.

Front: Work as for Back to 29 (33) cm or 11½" (13¾"). Cast off center 12 (14) sts and work on each side separately. At neck edge on every 2nd R cast off 2 sts 2 times and 1 st 4 (6) times. Work straight to 34 (38) cm or 13½" (15"), then shape shoulder to match Back.

Sleeves: Work as for Cardigan, but work rib in pink and finish in white.

Finishing: Press lightly. Join seams. Using finer circular needle and blue, pick up and K 83 (93) sts around neck. Work 3 cm or 1¼" in K 1, P 1 rib. Cast off in rib. Sew in zipper.

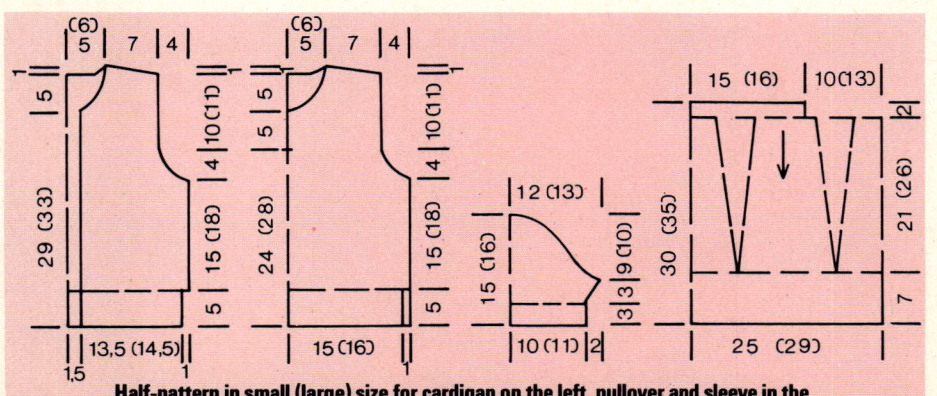

Half-pattern in small (large) size for cardigan on the left, pullover and sleeve in the center, and skirt on the right. Numbers are centimeters; inches are in the directions.

Best friends

Little girls love pleated skirts that swing as they walk. Knit these styles in garter stitch, with or without straps, then team them up with colored socks and shirt for a super outfit. As the skirts are worked from top to bottom, they can be lengthened as required. The width is created by regular increases.

Size: Directions are given for a 6-year-old, 116 cm (45½") tall. Changes for an 8-year-old, 128 cm (50½") tall are in brackets.

Materials Required:

Wide-striped Skirt: 50 (100) gm or 2 (4) oz each navy, red, green, and orange. **Narrow-striped Skirt:** 150 (200) gm or 6 (8) oz navy, 25 gm or 1 oz red, green, orange, and yellow [50 gm = 140 m or 153 yds]. Knitting needles and circular needle size 2 (Am) or 11 (Eng). Elastic for waist.

Basic Pattern: As given in the directions.

Color Sequence 1: *6 rnds each orange, green, red, and navy, repeat from *.

Color Sequence 2: *4 rnds navy, 2 rnds orange, 4 rnds navy, 2 rnds green, 4 rnds navy, 2 rnds yellow, 4 rnds navy, 2 rnds red, repeat from *.

Tension: 22 sts and 44 rnds = 10 cm or 4".

Abbreviations: K = knit. P = purl. St(s) = stitch(es). Rnd(s) = round(s).

DIRECTIONS

Begin at waist edge. Using circular needle, cast on 132 (156) sts in navy and work 2 cm or ¾" in rnds of K 1, P 1 rib. Now work in the required Color Sequence, working in pattern thus: **Rnd 1:** *K 5, P 1, repeat from * 21 (25) times more. **Rnd 2:** *P 2, K 1, P 5, K 1, P 3, repeat from * 10 (12) times more. **Rnd 3:** *K into front and back of 1st st, K 2, increase in next st as before, K 1, P 1, repeat from * all around — 176 (208) sts. **Rnd 4:** *P 3, K 1, P 4, repeat from * all around. **Rnd 5:** *K 7, P 1, repeat from * all around.

Repeat Rnds 4 and 5 7 times more, then Rnd 4 again. Now increase in next rnd as for Rnd 3, allowing for extra K sts in each repeat of pattern, thus increasing 44 (52) sts in rnd. Increase in the same way on every 18th rnd 5 (6) times more — 440 (572) sts.

Continue straight in pattern to 26 (30) cm or 10½" (11") from waist or length required. Cast off in pattern.

Straps: (make 2) Using knitting needles, cast on 7 sts and work in garter st for 55 (65) cm or 21½" (22"). Cast off.

Finishing: Sew elastic to inner waist edge. Sew on Straps.

One skirt has narrow stripes and straps, the other has broader stripes and no straps although these can be added if you wish to complete the look.

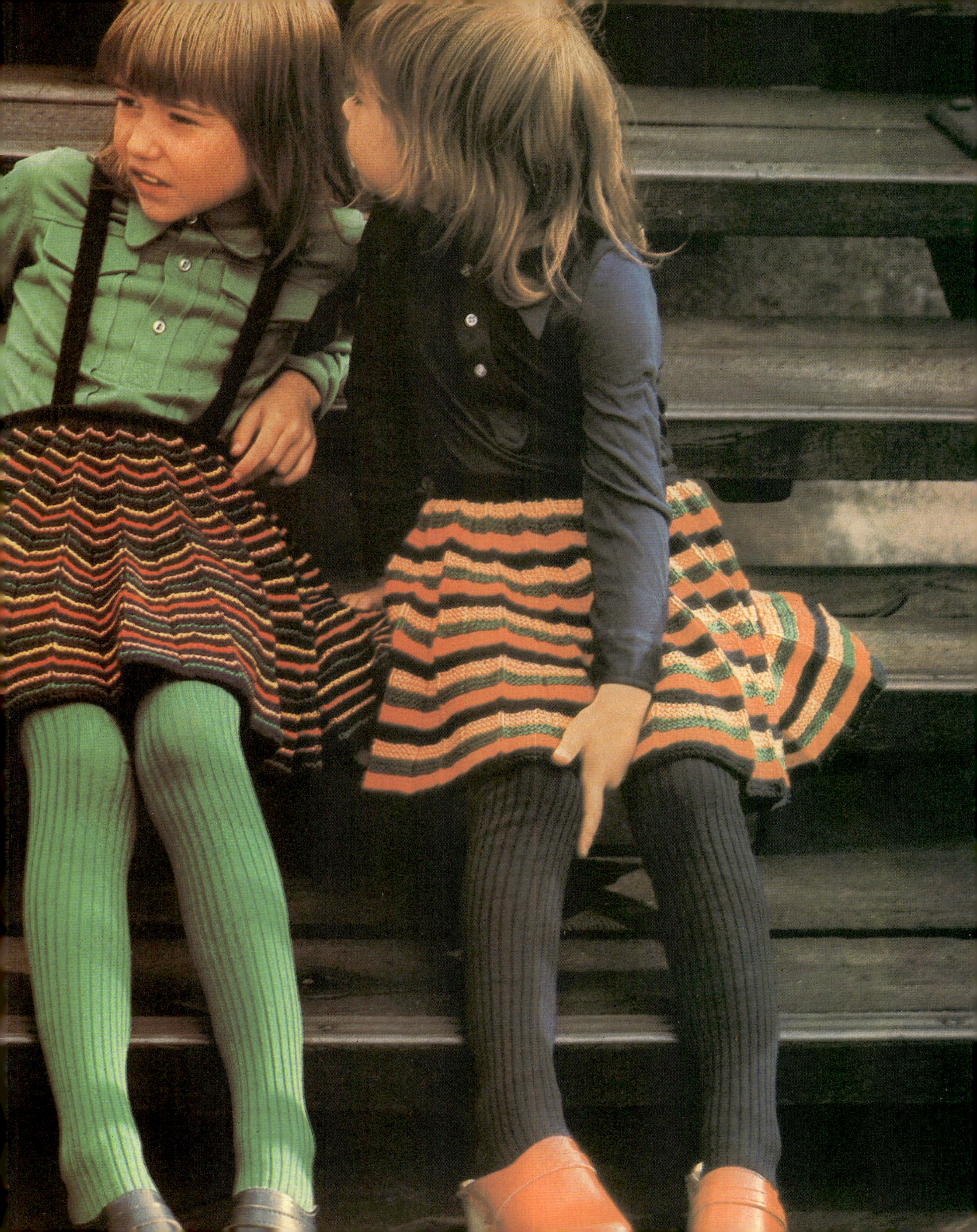

Transform your outfits with this crocheted mohair stole. It's long enough to wear as a filmy scarf, as a loose belt for a special dress, or as a light evening wrap-around.

Size: 160 cm x 60 cm or 63" x 23½".

Materials Required:

40 gm or 2 oz each grey, violet, rose, red, and dark red [40 gm = 475 m or 520 yds]. Crochet hook size H.

Basic Pattern: R 1: (wrong side) 1 sc in the 2nd st from hook, *5 ch, skip 3 sts, 1 sc in next st, repeat from * to end. R 2: Turn with 3 ch, *2 dc in 2nd ch of next loop, 1 dc in 3rd ch, 2 dc in 4th ch (this makes 5 dc in 3 ch of loop), 3 ch, 1 sc in center ch of following loop, 3 ch, repeat from *, ending 1 dc in last sc. R 3: Turn with 1 ch, 1 sc in 1st dc, *5 ch, 1 sc in the ch before the dc group, 5 ch, 1 sc in ch after the dc group, repeat from *. R 4: Turn with 6 ch, *1 sc in the center ch of the next loop, 3 ch, 5 dc (as before) into the center 3 ch of the next loop, 3 ch, repeat from *, ending 1 dc in last sc. R 5: Turn with 1 ch, 1 sc in the 1st dc, *5 ch, 1 sc in the ch after the dc, 5 ch, 1 sc into the ch before the next dc, repeat from *, but work last sc in the 4th turning ch. Repeat R 2–5.

Color Sequence: Foundation R and next 2 R in grey, *2 R each in violet, rose, red, dark red, and grey, repeat from * 4 times more.

Tension: 16 sts (2 repeats of pattern) and 8 R = 10 cm or 4".

Abbreviations: Ch = chain. Sc = single crochet. Dc = double crochet. St(s) = stitch(es). R = row(s).

DIRECTIONS
Using grey, make 258 ch and work in Basic Pattern and Color Sequence until repeats of Color Sequence are completed, then work 1 R in grey as for 5th R, but work only 3 ch in place of every 5 ch. Fasten off.

Finishing: Pin out and steam. Work a knotted fringe along each short end, using 10 strands for each knot and matching the color of each R end.

Choose subtle shades for an effective result. The colors should echo the softness of the yarn and the fineness of the stitches.

Fine as a cobweb

Crochet

Flowery netting

Our shawl is worked with many colors, but it can also be made in just one or two colors.

Size: 125 cm x 150 cm or 49" x 59".

Materials Required: 100 gm or 4 oz black for joining. 600 gm or 22 oz assorted colors for rosettes. [50 gm = 158 m or 172 yds]. Crochet hook size E.

Tension: Diameter of flower: 17 cm or $6\frac{3}{4}$".

Abbreviations: St(s) = stitch(es). R = row(s). Rnd(s) = round(s). Sc = single crochet. Ch = chain. Sl st = slip stitch.

DIRECTIONS

Rosette 1: Make 4 ch and join into a ring with a sl st. (Join all rounds with a sl st and begin each one with 1 ch as 1st sc.)
Rnd 1: Work 8 sc into ring. **Rnd 2:** Work 2 sc into each sc — 16 sts. **Rnd 3:** *1 sc into next sc, 2 sc in following sc, repeat from * all around. **Rnd 4:** *1 sc in next 2 sc, 2 sc in following sc, repeat from * all around. **Rnd 5:** *1 sc in each of next 3 sc, 2 sc in following sc, repeat from * all around. **Rnd 6:** *1 sc in each of next 2 sc, 1 ch, repeat from * all around. **Rnd 7:** *1 sc in ch, 18 ch, repeat from * all around. **Rnd 8:** With black, *1 sc into center of 18-ch loop, 6 ch, repeat from * all around. Fasten off.

Diagram for joining motifs: Three loops of adjacent motifs are joined with chain stitches and single crochet.

Rosette 2: Work this 2nd rosette as for Rosette 1 to end of Rnd 7. **Rnd 8:** With black, *1 sc into center of 18-ch loop, 3 ch, 1 sc into a 6-ch loop of adjacent rosette, 3 ch, repeat from * twice more, then end as for Rnd 8 of Rosette 1.
Make 75 more rosettes as Rosette 2, joining them in rows which are alternately 9 and 8 rosettes wide. Make sure there are 9 rosettes in 1st and last R and that they are all joined at the corresponding loops (see diagram at left).

Finishing: When all rosettes are connected there will be spaces at end of alternate R because of staggered flower pattern. Join black yarn to loose loop closest to end of short R. Work 6 ch, then 1 sc into corresponding loose loop of rosette on other side of space. Work 3 more ch loops in same way, but work 1 extra ch each time.

Flowers in crochet

Flowers to create an air of springtime

Now you can have springtime all year with these pillows decked with colorful blooms. The pillow covers are in crocheted mesh; the flowers and leaves are worked separately and sewn on in sprays, garlands, or clusters. Use the same idea for a bedcover with blooms strewn across the cover or arranged in the center.

Crochet

OVAL PILLOW

Size: 50 cm x 36 cm or 19½" x 14".

Materials Required: 150 gm or 6 oz white cotton, small amounts of cotton in red, lilac, purple, pink, turquoise, blue, dark green, and bright green. Crochet hook size D. Pillow.

Basic Pattern: 5 ch, 1 sc. In every round work the sc into ch loop of previous round.

Abbreviations: St(s) = stitch(es). Sc = single crochet. Dc = double crochet. Ch = chain. Rnd(s) = round(s). R = row(s).

DIRECTIONS

Pillow cover (make 2): Using white, make 41 ch and work 1 sc into 11th ch from hook, * 5 ch, 1 sc into 6th st from last sc, repeat from * 4 times more. Now continue to work around these loops. Mark the center, with a colored thread woven crosswise over center.

Rnd 2: Into 1st loop, work (5 ch, 1 sc) 2 times, then 5 ch, 1 sc into next 5 loops (end reached), turn piece lengthwise and into same loop work 2 more (5 ch, 1 sc) loops, work in Basic Pattern along other side, then work 2 more (5 ch, 1 sc) into end loop — 4 loops each end.

Rnd 3: Work Basic Pattern, working 2 loops into loops at each corner.

Rnds 4, 6, 8 and 9: Work in Basic Pattern.

Rnd 5: Work in Basic Pattern, working 2 loops into loop on either side of the center loop at each end.

Rnd 7: Work in Basic Pattern, working 2 loops in 2nd loop either side of the center loop at ends.

Rnd 10: Work 4 dc into each loop all around, and join rnd with a slip st.

Rnd 11: Work in dc, working 2 dc in every 2nd dc, but only working 1 dc on center 9 dc (marked crosswise) each side. **Rnd 12:** Work in Basic Pattern, working the sc into every 3rd dc. **Rnds 13, 14, and 15:** Work Basic Pattern. **Rnd 16:** Keeping center 6 loops on each side as 5 ch, 1 sc, work in pattern of 6 ch, 1 sc. **Rnds 17, 19, and 21:** Repeat Rnd 16. **Rnd 18:** Repeat Rnd 16, but work 7 ch, 1 sc instead of 6 ch, 1 sc. **Rnd 20:** Work in pattern, increasing all loops by 1 ch. **Rnds 22 and 23:** Repeat Rnd 16, but work 9 ch, 1 sc instead of 6 ch, 1 sc. Fasten off.

Flowers: Make 5 ch and join into a ring with a slip st.

Rnd 1: (1 sc, 3 ch) 4 times into ring, join with slip st. **Rnd 2:** With 3 ch as 1st dc, work 6 dc into each 3 – ch loop, join with a slip st. Fasten off.

Rnd 3: Working into the back of Rnd 1, * 6 ch, 1 sc around next sc at back of 1st round, repeat from * 2 times more, 6 ch, join with a slip st to 1st sc.

Rnd 4: With 3 ch as 1st dc, work 14 dc into each 6 – ch loop, join with slip st. Fasten off.

Work 36 flowers in various colors.

Leaves: Using either dark green or bright green, make 10 ch.

Leaf 1: 1 sc into 2nd ch from hook, 1 dc on each of next 6 ch, 1 sc on last ch. Fasten off.

Leaf 2: Using other green, make 9 ch and work 1 sc into 2nd ch from hook, 6 dc, then work 1 sc into tip of 1st leaf. Fasten off. Make 36 leaf pairs. To make a three-leaf cluster, work Leaf 2 twice.

Sew leaves to flowers, then sew flowers to cover. Begin on the dc ring, and sew them in a double row close together. Place the two pillow covers, wrong sides facing, and crochet together thus: work 1 sc around 2 edge loops, *6 ch, 1 sc around next 2 loops, repeat from *, joining pieces together until ¾ way round, then insert pillow and continue to close opening.

SQUARE PILLOW

Size: 40 cm x 40 cm or 16" x 16".

Materials Required: Yarn: See sample for Oval Pillow. 150 gm or 6 oz white cotton, small amounts of cotton in red, blue, yellow, green, and light green. Crochet hook size D. Pillow.

Basic Pattern and Abbreviations: See Oval Pillow.

DIRECTIONS

Pillow cover (make 2): Using white, make 5 ch and join into a ring with a slip st. **Rnd 1:** With 3 ch as 1st dc, work (5 dc, 1 ch) 4 times, join with a slip st.

Rnd 2: *1 dc on each of 5 dc, then 2 dc, 1 ch, 2 dc into 1 ch space, repeat from *3 times more, join with a slip st.

Continue to repeat Rnd 2, working 1 dc on dc and 2 dc, 1 ch, 2 dc into each of the ch at corners until side edge measures 20 cm or 8". Continue in loop pattern thus: work *5 ch, skip 2 dc, 1 sc into next dc, repeat from * all around, but work two 5-ch loops into corner ch. In next rnd work 5 ch, 1 sc into each loop, working 2 loops into corner loop. Continue thus until side of square measures 38 cm or 15", then work 1 rnd of 3 ch instead of 5 ch. In next rnd, work 3 dc into each 3-ch loop. In last rnd, work dc on dc. Fasten off.

Flowers and Leaves: Work 7 flowers each in red, yellow, and blue and make 21 sets of leaves, following directions for Oval Pillow. Sew leaves to flowers and sew flowers onto center of square.

Crochet the 2 pieces together on 3 sides as for Oval Pillow. Insert pillow, then crochet last side.

ROUND PILLOW

Size: 40 cm or 16" in diameter.

Materials Required: Yarn: See sample for Oval Pillow. 100 gm or 4 oz white cotton, small amounts of cotton in turquoise, purple, lilac, blue, pink, yellow, red, dark green, and bright green. Crochet hook size D. Pillow.

Basic Pattern and Abbreviations: See Oval Pillow.

DIRECTIONS

Pillow cover (make 2): Using white, make 6 ch and join into a ring with a slip st. **Rnd 1:** 12 dc into ring. **Rnds 2 and 3:** 2 dc in dc. **Rnds 4, 6 and 8:** Dc on dc. **Rnd 5:** Dc, working 2 dc on every 2nd dc. **Rnd 7:** Dc working 2 dc on every 3rd dc. **Rnd 9:** Dc, working 2 dc on every 4th dc — 120 sts. Continue in loop pattern thus: **Rnd 10:** *4 ch, skip 2 dc, 1 sc in next dc, repeat from * all around, then slip – st along to center of loop. **Rnd 11:** *4 ch, 1 sc in center of next loop, repeat from * all around. Continue thus but in next and every 2nd rnd, work 1 more ch each time (i.e. Rnd 12 will have 5 ch instead of 4). Continue until Rnd 22 has been worked. Fasten off.

Flowers and Leaves: Make 20 flowers of mixed colors and 20 two- and three-leaf clusters, following directions for Oval Pillow. Sew the leaves to the flowers and the flowers on dc stitches. Finish as for Oval Pillow.

How-to

Crocheting flowers and leaves

The photograph on the left shows a finished flower with leaves.
Directions: Make 5 chain stitches, then join them into a ring with a slip stitch. Round 1: Make 1 chain, * 1 single crochet, make 3 chains, repeat from * 3 times, then close the round with a slip stitch.

1 Round 2: Make 3 chain stitches, work 5 double crochets around the first chain-stitch loop, then work 6 double crochets around all following loops, close with a slip stitch.

2 The chain-stitch loops of the next round are worked into the back of Round 1. Round 3: Make 2 chain stitches and fasten to back of single crochet in Round 1 with slip stitch.

3 Make 1 chain, *make 6 chains, 1 single crochet into the middle of the 6 double crochets worked around the chain-stitch loop, repeat from * 3 times, close round with slip stitch.

4 Round 4: Make 3 chain stitches, work 13 double crochets around the first chain-stitch loop, then work 14 double crochets into all following loops, close with slip stitch.

5 Leaf 1: Make 10 chains, 1 single crochet in the 2nd chain from hook, then work 6 double and 1 single crochets.

6 Leaf 2: Make 9 chains; work 1 single crochet in the 2nd chain from hook, 6 double and 1 single crochets into Leaf 1.

How-to

Loop crochet

1 Loops are worked from wrong side and lie on right side. Work 1 row sc, turn. Make 1 sc into 1st st, draw yarn through next st, then wind yarn from front to back over a flat batten.

2 Draw yarn, now lying behind the batten, through both sts on the hook. Work 1 loop into every following sc, to last sc, work 1 sc and turn with 1 ch. All right side R are in sc.

3 <u>Color change on wrong side R</u>: Insert hook into next st, draw through first color, now place new color onto piece and wind around batten, yarn over hook and draw through both sts. Ends are sewn in later.

4 <u>Color change on right side R</u>: Insert hook into last st of color, yarn over hook and draw through, now pick up new color, yarn over hook and draw through both loops on hook.

Geometric patterns crocheted in loops make highly individual cushions that will suit many furnishings.

For all cushions
Materials Required:

[50 gm = 175 m or 191 yds]. Colors and quantities are given in individual directions. Crochet hook size 7. A flat batten or piece of cardboard 3 cm or 1¼" wide. Fabric for cushion backs.

Basic Stitch 1: Sc. Every R begins with 1 ch, then sc in 1st st and every st to end.

Basic Stitch 2: Loop crochet. R 1: (right side) Sc, turn with 1 ch. R 2: See photographs 1 and 2 of How-to. Repeat R 1 and 2.

Tension: About 15 sts and 15 R = 10 cm or 4".

Abbreviations: Ch = chain. Sc = single crochet. St(s) = stitch(es). R = row(s). Rnd(s) = round(s).

Finishing: Cut the fabric to size of cushion, sew to crocheted part, leaving one end open, insert cushion, then sew up seam.

Left Cushion
<u>Size:</u> 40 cm or 16" square.
<u>Yarn Required:</u> 100 gm or 4 oz each of copper and olive, 50 gm or 2 oz each of dark green, orange, and turquoise.

DIRECTIONS
Work the center squares first. Using orange, make 12 ch, join on dark green and work 12 ch, turn with 1 ch. Work dark green in sc and orange in loop st. (For color changes, see photographs 3 and 4 of How-to). Work 14 R, then reverse colors and work another 14 R. Now work all around the square in sc using turquoise, working 24 sc each side and 3 sc into corner sc. Work 13 more rnds in sc, working 3 sc into each corner sc. Now work 14 rnds in Basic Stitch 2, but only increase at corners on sc rnds, work first in copper, then in olive.

<u>Shaping corner on loop rnd:</u> Work to corner, work loop in 1st corner sc, 1 sc on center sc, then take the batten and begin next side, working 2 loops into 3rd corner sc.

Right Cushion
<u>Size:</u> 40 cm or 16" square.
<u>Yarn Required:</u> 100 gm or 4 oz each of copper and olive, 50 gm or 2 oz each of dark green, orange and turquoise.

DIRECTIONS
First work the center orange square. Make 12 ch, turn with 1 ch and work 14 R. Now work around the square in an L shape in turquoise: fasten the yarn to 1st st of last orange R, make 12 ch, turn with 1 ch and work back along the ch in sc, work across last R of orange, turn corner, then work 12 sc along side of square, turn and work 7 more R in sc, then work 8 R of loop pattern, shaping corners as given for previous cushion. For the matching dark green L-shaped area, fasten the yarn into the 1st st worked on last turquoise R, work 12 sc along the narrow turquoise R ends, 12 sc along orange foundation edge, and 12 sc along other free side of orange square, turn. Work 7 more R in sc and 8 R in loop st, always slip-stitching each R to the turquoise ch – R. Work 2 more L shapes of sc and

Cushion yourself

loop pattern, one in olive and one in rust in the positions shown in the photograph.

Lower Center Cushion

Size: 55cm x 45cm or 21½" x 17¾".

Yarn Required: 200gm or 8oz turquoise, 50gm or 2oz each dark green, gold, copper, olive, and pale blue.

DIRECTIONS

This cushion is worked in 3 parts. Center Strip: Make 23 ch in each of turquoise, olive and again turquoise, turn with 1 ch. Work turquoise sts in loop st for 50 R and on the center 23 sts work 10 R each of olive, pale blue, dark green, pale blue, and olive in sc. Fasten off.

Side Strip: (make 2) Make 23 ch using gold and turn with 1 ch. Work 10 R of sc in gold, copper, and olive, then 26 R in turquoise in loop st. Now work 10 R each of olive, copper, and gold in sc. Sew pieces in position as shown in picture.

Top Center Cushion

Size: 55cm x 45cm or 21½" x 17¾".

Yarn Required: 100gm or 4oz each of dark green, orange and turquoise, 50 gm or 2oz copper.

DIRECTIONS

Make 12 ch consecutively in turquoise, orange, turquoise, copper, turquoise, orange; and turquoise, turn with 1 ch – 84 sts.

R 1–18: Work turquoise sts in sc, the other colors in loop st. R 19–34: Work 36 sts each side in loop st using dark green, the center 12 sts in loop st with copper. R 35–52: Repeat R 1–18. R 53–68: 12 sts each in dark green and orange, center 36 sts in dark green, 12 sts each orange and dark green – all in loop st. R 69–86: Repeat R 1–18. Finally, cut loops open.

1713

Take your place

With our sturdy mats, crocheted in plait stitch, using dyed cotton string.

Size: 45 x 35 cm or 17¾" x 13¾".
Materials Required:
380 gm or 14 oz white [40 gm = 25 m or 27 yds]. Crochet hook size J. Green or orange dye.
Basic Stitch: Plait stitch in continuous rnds. **Rnd 1:** Sc. **Rnd 2 and all following Rnds:** Sc, but with the hook inserted at back of work into the lower horizontal thread between sts (small photograph). This pushes the 2 upper threads to the front.
Tension: 13 sts and 16 rnds = 10 cm or 4".
Abbreviations: Ch = chain. Sc = single crochet. St(s) = stitch(es). Rnd(s) = round(s).
Note: Wind off about 20 gm or 1 oz and dye the remainder in color of choice.

Plait stitch is worked into the lower horizontal thread at the back of the piece.

DIRECTIONS

Begin at center. Make 14 ch, turn.
R 1: Beginning in 2nd ch from hook, make 12 sc, 3 sc in last st, turn work and continue along other side of foundation ch, then work 3 sc in turning ch. Continue in Basic Stitch, shaping thus:
Rnd 2: Work 3 sc in 1st and 3rd sc to form 2 corners at each end.
Rnd 3: Work 3 sc in center sc of 3-sc groups. **Rnd 4:** Repeat Rnd 3.
Rnd 5: Sc in sc, without increasing.
Rnd 6: Work 3 sc in 1st sc of 3 sc at right corner, then 3 sc into last sc of 3 sc at left corner. Repeat at other end. **Rnds 7 and 8:** Repeat Rnd 3.
Continue to repeat Rnds 5–8 until place mat measures about 45 cm x 35 cm or 17¾" x 13¼" — or size required, working last 3 rnds as 2 rnds white and 1 rnd in color. Fasten off.

Right on target

These original pullovers are crocheted in a square from the center outward.

Size: Directions are for 64 cm or 25" chest. Changes for 69 cm or 27" chest are in brackets.

Materials Required:

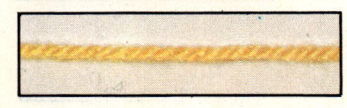

200 (250) gm or 8 (9) oz yellow or green, 50 (100) gm or 2 (4) oz white [50 gm = 140 m or 153 yds]. Crochet hook size E.

Basic Stitch: Dc. Every R begins with 2 ch, 1 dc in 1st st and ends on last st. Every rnd begins with 3 ch, then turn, work in dc as given in directions, and join each rnd with a slip st.

Color Sequence: Alternately 1 rnd white and 1 rnd yellow or green.

Tension: 18 sts and 10 R = 10 cm or 4".

Abbreviations: Ch = chain. Dc = double crochet. St(s) = stitch(es). R = row(s). Rnd(s) = round(s).

DIRECTIONS

Back: First work 1 square. Rnd 1: Using yellow or green, make 4 ch and work 15 dc in 1st st, join with a slip st. Rnd 2: (right side) Join on white. 3 ch, turn, and work 2 dc in slip st, *1 dc in each of next 3 dc, 5 dc in next st (corner). Repeat from * twice more, then 1 dc in each of last 3 sts, 2 dc in slip st — 4 corners formed. Rnd 3: Join on yellow or green, 3 ch, turn, and work in dc, working 5 dc in 3rd of 5 dc groups at corner, but working 1st and last corners as in Rnd 2.

Repeat Rnd 3 until the 8th (9th) yellow or green stripe from beginning has been worked.

Now work the plain border onto 1 side of the square. Counting from corner to corner, work 61 (69) dc. Work dc on dc in yellow or green for 10 (11) cm or 4" (4¼"). Fasten off.

Front: Work a square as for Back.

Sleeves: Join the squares at shoulders for 7 (8) cm or 2¾" (3") each side.

Now, using yellow or green, work 30 (34) dc from side center of square to shoulder and 30 (34) dc down to corresponding point on other side.

Work dc on dc, decreasing 1 st each end of every 5th (4th) R 6 (8) times — 48 (52) sts *At the same time,* at 27 (31) cm or 10½" (12½"), work 1 R each white, yellow or green, white, then 2 R yellow or green, and fasten off.

Finishing: Join sleeve and side seams. Press seams.

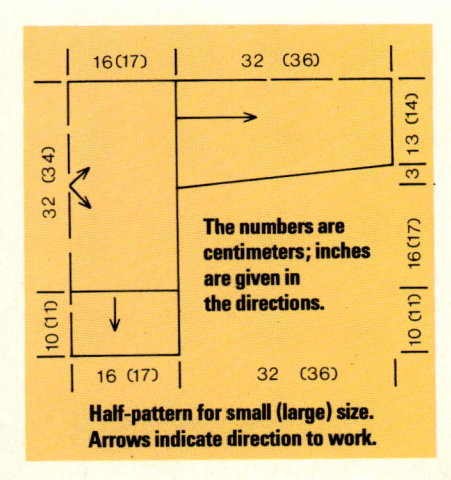

Half-pattern for small (large) size. Arrows indicate direction to work.

The numbers are centimeters; inches are given in the directions.

Lollipop stripes

For Both
Materials Required:

Quantities and colors are given in individual directions. Crochet hook size D.
Basic Stitch: Dc. Each R begins after 2 turning ch in 1st st and ends on last st.
Tension: 23 sts and 12 R = 10 cm or 4".
Abbreviations: Ch = chain. R = row(s). St(s) = stitch(es). Sc = single crochet. Dc = double crochet.

Woman's Pullover
Size: Directions are for 84 cm or 33" bust. Changes for 92 cm or 36" bust are in brackets.
Yarn: 200 (250) gm or 8 (9) oz white, 50 gm or 2 oz each of turquoise, blue, purple, lilac, pink, red, pale green, and dark green.
Color Sequence: Beginning on a right side R, work 3 (5) R white; 2 R each dark green, pale green, white, red, pink, white, purple, lilac, white, blue, and turquoise; 1 R white.

DIRECTIONS
Right Back/Sleeve: Begin at side seam and make 125 ch. Work in dc and Color Sequence, but increase for Sleeve by working 5 dc in the 37th st from right edge. Work dc in dc, working 5 dc in center dc of 5-dc group on every R. Work until Color Sequence is completed, ending 1 R in white. Fasten off.
Left Back/Sleeve: Work as for Right Back/Sleeve, but in reverse, increasing in R 1 in the 87th st from right edge. Then after the 3 (5) white R, begin with turquoise and work Color Sequence in reverse, ending with dark green, then work 1 R white. Fasten off.
Left Front/Sleeve: Work as for Right Back/Sleeve to end of purple stripe then at increase st, leave right-hand sts unworked and work straight on remaining sts, following Color Sequence and ending 1 R white. Fasten off.
Right Front/Sleeve: Work as for Left Front/Sleeve, reversing increases as for Left Back, working Color Sequence in reverse, and ending 1 R white.
Finishing: Dampen parts, pin them out, and leave to dry. Join seams from the right side, keeping work flat. Using white, work 3 R of sc, working 2 sc in each R of dc and working 3 sts together in each corner at neck edge.

Child's Pullover
Size: Directions are for 62–64 cm or 24"–25" chest.
Yarn: 100 gm or 4 oz white. Small amounts of turquoise, blue, red, pink, pale green, and dark green.
Color Sequence: Beginning on a wrong side R, work 2 R each white, dark green, light green, white, red, pink, white, blue, and turquoise; work 1 R white.

DIRECTIONS
Right Back/Sleeve: Begin at side seam and make 85 ch. Work in dc and Color Sequence and increase for Sleeve by working 5 dc in the 55th st from left edge (lower edge). Work dc in dc, but work 5 dc in center dc of 5-dc group on every R. Work until Color Sequence is completed. Fasten off.
Left Back/Sleeve: Work in reverse, increasing in R 1 in the 29th st from left edge and after the 2 R in white, work Color Sequence in reverse. Fasten off.
Left Front/Sleeve: Work as for Right Back/Sleeve to end of red stripe then at increase st, leave neck edge sts unworked and work straight on remaining sts, following the Color Sequence. Fasten off.
Right Front/Sleeve: Work as for Left Front/Sleeve, reversing increase as for Left Back/Sleeve and working Color Sequence in reverse. Fasten off.
Finishing: See Woman's Pullover.

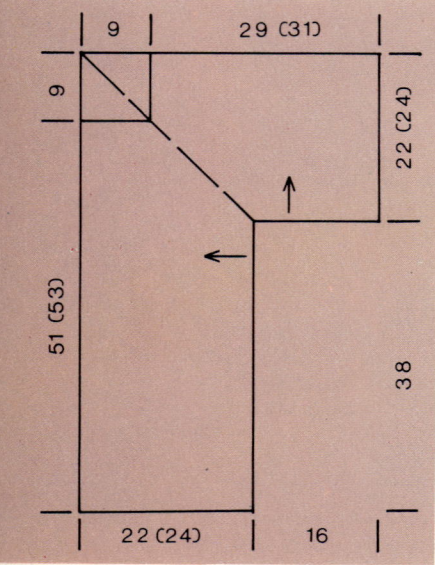

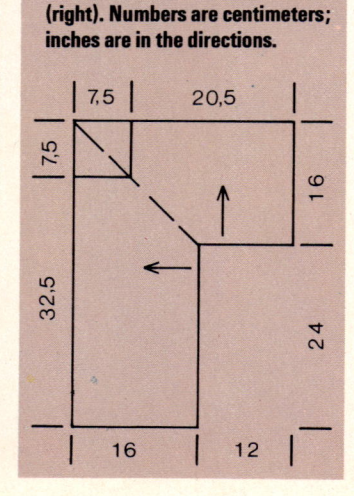

Half-pattern in small (large) size for the woman (left) and the child (right). Numbers are centimeters; inches are in the directions.

When you crochet our super striped top for yourself, your little girl is bound to want one too. Wear it over a plain blouse which picks out one of the colors in the stripes.

Showing their true stripes

Perfect with casual shirts, these sleeveless V-neck pullovers are a useful addition to a boy's wardrobe. They are worked in afghan crochet and one style is striped throughout, while the other has a few bands of color to highlight the neck, armholes, and waist. The bands are worked in single crochet.

FOR BOTH STYLES

Size: Directions are for 66 cm or 26" chest. Changes for 70 cm or 27½" chest are in brackets.

Materials Required:

100 (150) gm or 4 (6) oz blue and 50 gm or 2 oz each of white and navy *or* 150 gm or 6 oz green and small amounts of orange and white [50 gm = 190 m or 200 yds]. Crochet hook size D. Afghan crochet hook size 7.

Basic Pattern: Afghan cross-stitch. R 1: (right side) 1 ch, then draw a loop through every st. R 2: (return R) 1 ch, *draw a loop through 2 loops on hook, repeat from * to end. R 3: 1 ch, *draw a loop first from the 2nd then from the 1st loop of the previous right side R, thus crossing loops (see photograph), repeat from * to end. R 4: Repeat R 2. R 5: Repeat R 3, but move along 1 loop to right by drawing 1st loop from 1st st, then work from * of R 3 to last loop, draw loop from last st. Repeat R 2–5.

Color Sequence — Blue Pullover: *4 R blue, 1 R each (white, navy, blue) 2 times, 1 R white, 1 R navy, 4 R blue, 1 R each navy and white, repeat from *.

Color Sequence — Green Pullover: 8 R green, 1 R each (white, orange, green) 2 times, 1 R white, 1 R orange, 4 R green, 1 R each orange, white, 4 R green, 1 R each (white, orange, green) 2 times, 1 R white, 1 R orange, and continue in green.

Tension: 25 sts and 32 R = 10 cm or 4".

Abbreviations: Ch = chain. Sc = single crochet. R = row(s). St(s) = stitch(es). Rnd(s) = round(s).

DIRECTIONS

Back: Using the crochet hook and blue or green, make 85 (91) ch and work in sc to 4 (6) cm or 1½" (2½") — 84 (90) sc. Change to the afghan hook and work in Basic Pattern and Color Sequence to 24 (27) cm or 9½" (10½").

Shape Armholes: At each end of every R, decrease 3 sts 1 time, 2 sts 2 times, and 1 st 5 times — 60 (66) sts. Work straight to 40 (44) cm or 15¾" (17").

Shape Neck and Shoulders: Leave 26 sts unworked and work on each side separately. At neck edge, in every 2nd R decrease 2 sts 2 times and 1 st 1 time. *At the same time,* at 41 (45) cm or 16" (17¾") at armhole edge, in every 2nd R decrease 6 (7) sts 1 time and 6 (8) sts 1 time.

Front: Work as for Back to 24 (27) cm or 9½" (10½"). Divide work at center and shape armhole as for Back. At neck edge, in every 2nd R decrease 2 sts 3 times, 1 st 6 times, and 1 st on every 4th R 6 times. Shape shoulder as for Back at 41 (45) cm or 15¾" (17").

Finishing: Press lightly. Join seams. With right side of work facing and using the crochet hook, work 130 (136) sc around neck. Use blue for Blue Pullover and for Green Pullover work 3 rnds green and 1 rnd each white and orange, then 2 rnds green. Work in sc, decreasing 1 sc on each rnd at center V, to 2.5 cm or 1". Fasten off. Work sc border in the same Color Sequence around armholes with 92 (98) sts.

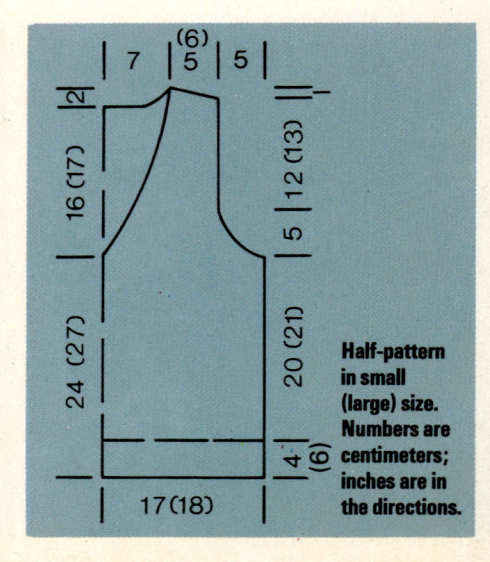

Half-pattern in small (large) size. Numbers are centimeters; inches are in the directions.

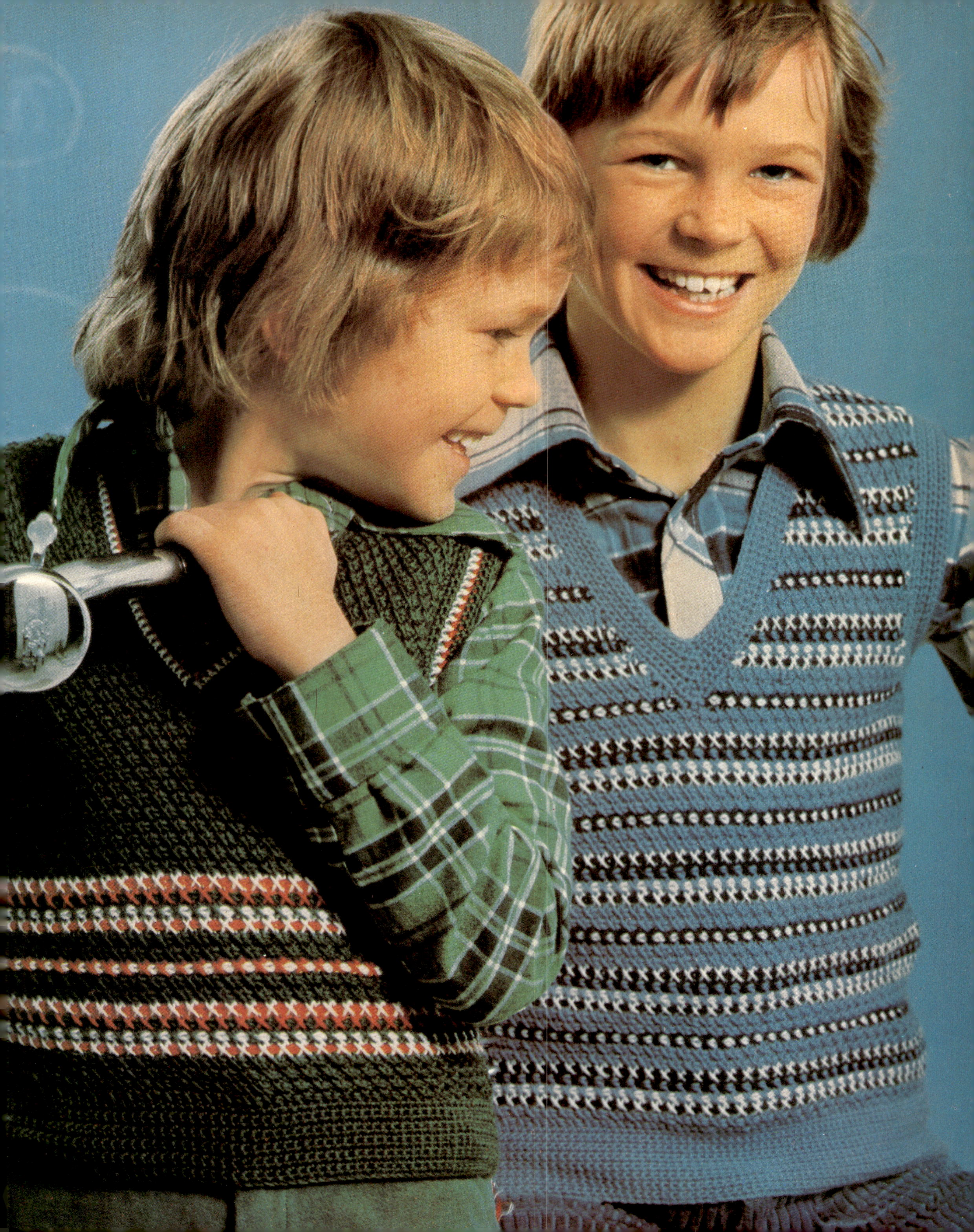

Extra special

For Both

Size: Directions are for 66 cm or 26" chest. Changes for 72 cm or 28" chest are in brackets.

Materials Required:

Quantities and colors are given in individual directions [50 gm = 161 m or 176 yds]. Crochet hook size 15. Afghan crochet hook size K. Knitting needles size 2. St holders.

Basic Pattern: Each R is a double R. R 1: (right side) Beginning in the 2nd st from the hook, draw 1 loop from each st, 1 ch, then loop off 2 sts at a time. R 2: Beginning without a ch and working into the 1st space between sts, draw a loop from each space of previous R, 1 ch, then loop off 2 sts at a time. R 3: Beginning without a ch and working into the 2nd space draw a loop from each space of previous R, draw last loop from last st, 1 ch, loop off 2 sts at a time. Repeat R 2 and 3.

Embroidery Pattern: See How-to. Use yarn double.

Tension: 20 sts and 22 R = 10 cm or 4".

Abbreviations: Ch = chain. Sc = single crochet. St = stitch. R = row.

Boy's Jacket

Additional Materials: 400 (450) gm or 15 (16) oz dark green. Remnants of white, yellow, pale green, and rust for the embroidery. Open-ended zipper: 40 (45) cm or 16" (18") long.

DIRECTIONS

Back: Using dark green and afghan hook, make 73 (77) ch and work in Basic Pattern to 21 cm or 8¼".

Shape Armholes: Decrease 10 sts each end by working sc over first 10 sts, pattern to last 10 sts, leave 52 (56) sts. Work straight to 37 (39) cm or 14½" (15¼"). Fasten off.

Left Front: Using dark green, make 37 (39) ch and work in Basic Pattern, shaping armhole as for Back, then continue straight to 32 (33) cm or 12½" (13"), ending at side edge.

Shape Neck: Decrease 3 sts at end of next R. On every 2nd R, decrease 2 sts 2 times and 1 st 3 times. Continue straight and fasten off at 37 (39) cm or 14½" (15¼").

Right Front: Work as for Left Front, reversing shapings.

Sleeves: Using dark green, make 49 (57) ch and work in Basic Pattern, increasing 1 st every 18th (20th) R 8 times — 64 (72) sts. Work straight to 39 (41) cm or 15¼" (16"). Fasten off.

Waistband: Using dark green and knitting needles, cast on 163 (175) sts and work 6 (8) cm or 2½" (3") in K 1, P 1 rib. Cast off in rib.

Cuffs: Using dark green and knitting needles, cast on 48 (54) sts and work 6 (8) cm or 2½" (3") in K 1, P 1 rib. Cast off in rib.

Collar: Using dark green and knitting needles, cast on 73 (79) sts and work in K 1, P 1 rib for 3 (4) cm or 1¼" (1½"). Cast off in rib.

Finishing: Press lightly. Using double yarn and working from lower edge to shoulder of Back and Fronts, work 1 stripe each in pale green, yellow, rust, white, and pale green. Leave 3 R between all following groups of stripes. Join all seams. Sew on Collar. Sew on all other knitted pieces, easing in the lower edges of main pieces. Now using the crochet hook, work 82 (90)

They'll play happily in their pretty jackets worked in afghan crochet. Contrasting strands are woven through to form colored bands.

The boy's green jacket has a front zipper and a stand-up collar.

The girl's brown version is buttoned at the front and has a turn-back collar.

Half-pattern in small (large) size for boy's jacket (left), sleeve (center), and girl's jacket (right). Numbers are centimeters; inches are given in the directions.

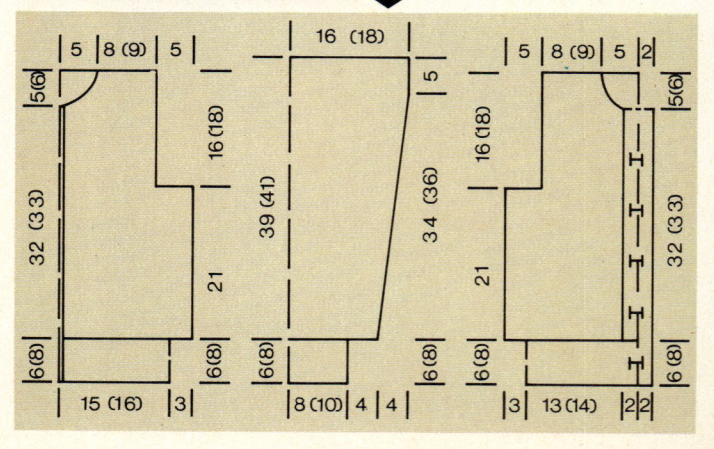

sc along each front edge. Fasten off. Sew zipper under this R of crochet.

Girl's Jacket

Additional Materials: 400 (450) gm or 15 (16) oz brown. Remnants of white, yellow, pale green, and rust for the embroidery. 8 buttons.

DIRECTIONS

Back: Using brown, work as for Back of Boy's Jacket.

Right Front: Make 33 (35) ch and work as for Boy's Jacket, but shape neck by decreasing 2 sts 1 time and 1 st 4 times.

Left Front: Work as for Right Front, reversing shapings.

Sleeves: Using brown, work as for Boy's Cardigan.

Waistband/Front Borders: Using brown and knitting needles, cast on 181 (193) sts and work in K 1, P 1 rib for 3 (4) cm or 1¼" (1½"), ending at front edge. In next R, cast off 8th–10th sts and in following R cast on 3 sts in place of those cast off. Work straight to 6 (8) cm or 2½" (3").
In next R, rib 13, cast off center 155 (167) sts, rib 13. Continue on each border separately in rib, working 4 more buttonholes in line with previous one at 7 (7.5) cm or 2¾" (3") intervals. Work straight to 38 (41) cm or 15" (16¼") and leave sts on st holders.

Finishing: Press lightly on wrong side. Embroider as for Boy's Jacket, but work 1 R each rust, pale green, white, yellow, and rust. Join all seams and sew on Waistband/Borders. Now with right side facing, rib across right Border sts, pick up 67 (73) sts around neck edge, then rib across left Border sts. Work in rib, working a buttonhole above previous one in next R and 2 more when Collar is 10 cm or 4" and 14 cm or 5½". Cast off at 16 cm or 6¼". Sew on buttons.

Embroidery on afghan crochet

How-to

Here we show you how the colored stripes are worked on the afghan crochet background. Use double yarn throughout.

1 Begin in the 4th R. Insert the needle under first 4 vertical threads, then *2 double R up insert the needle under the following 2 threads, then 2 double R down insert the needle under the next 4 threads. Repeat from *.

2 For the next R above, insert the needle under the 3 sts above the group of 4, then *2 double R higher insert the needle under only 1 st, and 2 double R down insert the needle under 3 sts. Repeat from *.

3 In the center R, the needle is inserted under 2 sts each time.

4 The 2 remaining R are worked in reverse from the first 2 R, so that when finished the drawn-through strands appear to lie under alternating triangles.

Suit yourself

Illustrated Sewing 53

Here we feature two mix-and-match suits with narrow skirts and smart, well-cut jackets. The patterns are in sizes C and E on Pattern Sheet 53.

Style 1 has a hip-length, gaberdine jacket with plenty of fashion detail. There is a notched collar, a gathered waist, patch pockets, and pockets in the side seams. The width at the back is gathered into a box pleat.
The straight-cut woollen skirt is fashionably long with a front pleat which also conceals the zipper.

Style 2 is designed along classic trenchcoat lines. The gaberdine jacket is double breasted and belted at the waist. The sleeves are raglan and are finished with buttoned tabs. The back view shows the inverted box pleat and the loose yoke buttoned down. The three front pockets finish the look. The straight skirt is in a subtle herringbone tweed. The pleat is at the side and is top-stitched to give a wrap-around effect.

A concealed coat zipper

First method

This is the simplest way to insert a covered zipper. However, the zipper tape is visible on the underlap when the garment is worn open.

1 Before beginning to insert the zipper, stitch on the upper part of the facing. Finish the cut edges of the facing and turn up the hem. Baste all the lines marked for inserting a zipper. On the right front, baste in the stitching line as marked on the pattern, then the center front and the fold line. Mark the center front line on the facing, too (see photograph 1a). On the left front, mark the center front and press the facing along the fold line (see photograph 1b).

2 Open up the zipper so that it is in two parts. On the right front edge, place one part of the zipper with the teeth along the marked line of the facing. Fold back the upper end and stitch down the length of the tape twice (see photograph 2a). On the left front, place the other part of the zipper with the teeth lying along the center front marking, then stitch through all layers twice in the same way (see photograph 2b).

3 On the right front edge, press along the fold line, then stitch along the marked stitching line. Photograph 3a shows the inserted zipper. Using this method, you can replace a damaged zipper quickly and easily.

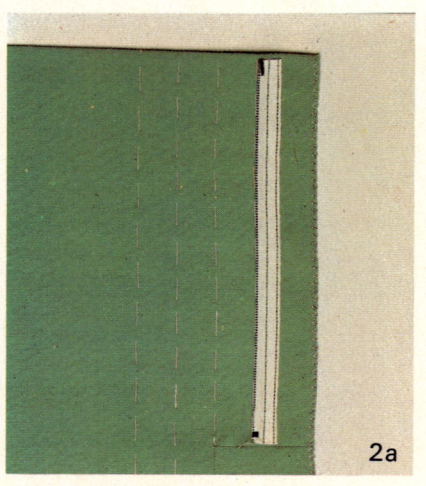

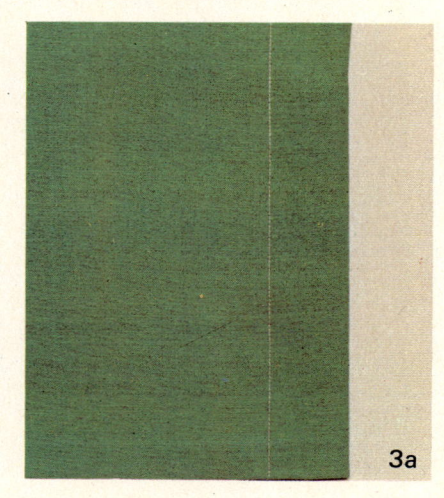

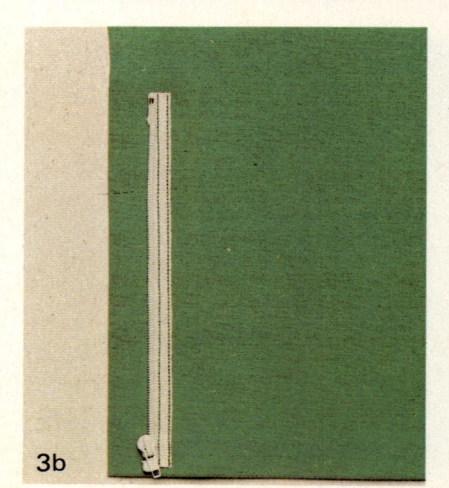

How-to

Second method

This second method involves working the right front as described for the first method. On the left front, the lower facing is not cut-in-one but, stitched on, and the tape is caught into the seamline.

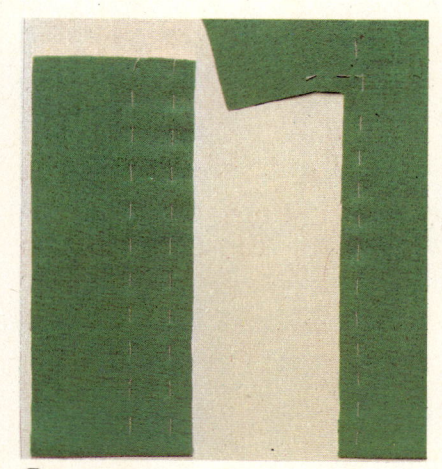

1 The photograph above shows the hem already turned up and the upper part of the facing stitched to the front. Mark the center front line and the fold line on the underlap as shown on the left. Mark center front and seamline for zipper (see above right).

2 Stitch the underlap horizontally to the front as shown above, working from the cut edge of the facing to the center front, and up to the seamline for the zipper allowing 0.5 cm ($\frac{1}{4}$") clearance for the toothed edge.

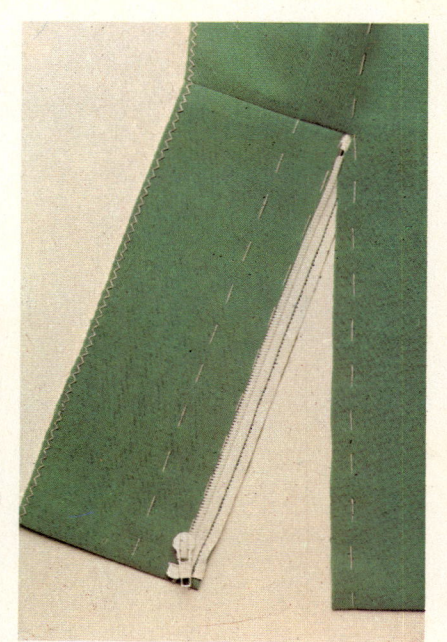

3 Place the toothed edge of the zipper tape to the center front of the underlap and stitch along the center of the tape. Clip diagonally into the corner of the seam allowance of the front. You will find that the upper end of the zipper will slip easily underneath.

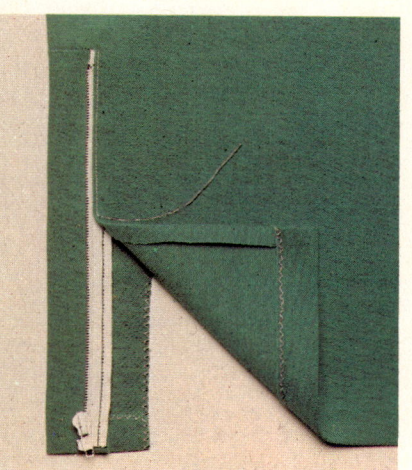

4 First press the facing along the fold line, then fold the seam allowance on the front edge to the inside and place the fold edge close to the teeth of the zipper. Stitch down through all layers carefully and neatly. The photograph above shows these two stages.

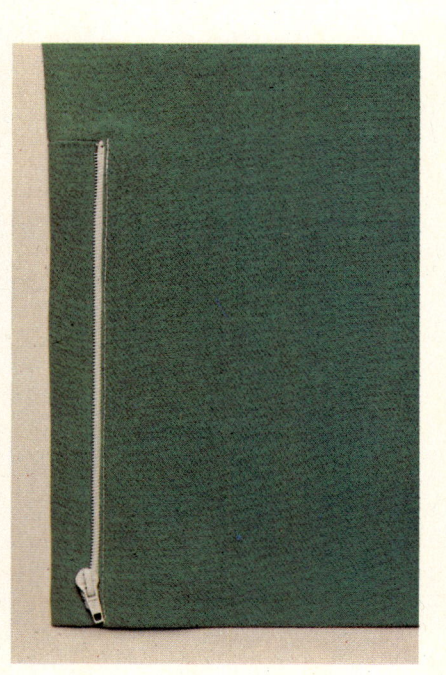

5 The photographs above show how the finished zipper will look on a garment. Following the method described above, the zipper is caught into the seam and is not visible from the right side.

Easy to sew, practical to wear — dungarees and a pinafore dress with matching hats made in hard-wearing striped cotton.

∗

Size: Chest: 52 cm (20½"). Height: 86 cm (34").
Note: The pattern pieces are given actual size on Pattern Sheet 53.

Pinafore dress and hat

Materials Required: Striped cotton: 1.30 m (1⅜ yds), 90 cm (36") wide. Iron-on non-woven interfacing: 0.30 m (⅜ yd), 82 cm (32") wide. 4 white buttons. 2 dungaree buckles with 3.5 cm (1⅜") bar.

Cutting out: Pinafore Dress: Take care to match the stripes when cutting out. Seam allowances: add 4 cm (1½") for the hem. At the pocket opening edges, add 3 cm (1¼"), elsewhere 1.5 cm (⅝"). The facings are marked on the upper front and back; the pockets are also marked on the front and can be traced off. For the straps, cut out 2 strips each 7 cm (2¾") wide and 15 cm (5⅞") long plus seam allowance.

Hat: Cut out the crown section 6 times in fabric and interfacing with 0.5 cm (¼") for the seams. Cut out the brim 4 times with allowances.

Sewing: Pinafore Dress: Press the pocket seam allowance under all around and top-stitch close to the edge at the sides. Work the buttonholes and sew on buttons, then stitch on the pocket along the upper and lower edges and the lower 2 cm (¾") of the open side edges.

Join the skirt side seams, also those of the facing. Stitch, turn, and top-stitch the straps close to the edge. Now stitch on the facings and turn, catching in the straps at the back where marked. Top-stitch all around the upper edges. Turn under the hem twice and stitch. Finally, sew buttons to the front and attach the buckles.

Hat: Iron on the interfacing and join the crown sections together, right sides facing, stitching from base to tip and finishing the seams. The brim is worked double. Stitch each part into a circle, then stitch both parts together around the outer edge. Turn and top-stitch close to the outer edge. Pin the brim to the crown with single fabric, right sides facing, and stitch. Then stitch down the inner edge of the brim along the seamline from the right side.

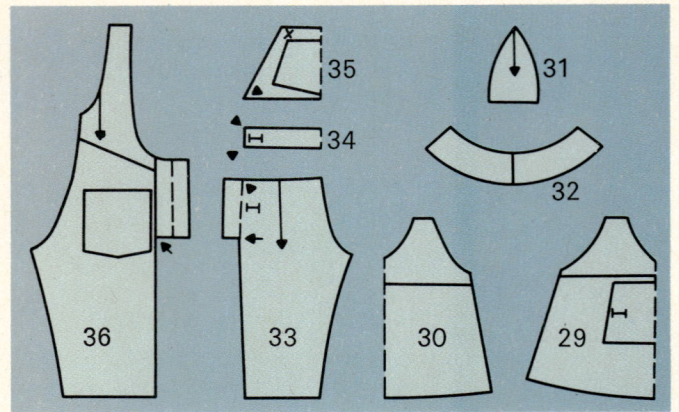

▲ **The dungarees have straps which button at the front and patch pockets on the bib and back.**

▶ **Team this pretty little pinafore dress with colored socks and pullovers or T-shirts.**

◀ **The pattern pieces shown here are given actual size on Pattern Sheet 53.**

Dungarees and hat

Materials Required: Striped cotton: 1.80 m (2 yds), 90 cm (36") wide. Iron-on non-woven interfacing: 0.30 m (⅜ yd), 82 cm (32") wide. 6 white buttons. 2 dungaree buckles with 3.5 cm (1⅜") bar.

Cutting out: Dungarees: Take care to match the stripes when cutting out. Seam allowances: add 2 cm (¾") to the upper edges of the pockets, 4 cm (1⅝") at the hem, 1.5 cm (⅝") elsewhere. The upper facing and pocket of the pants back and bib pocket can be traced from the pattern piece. Cut out the bib and front waistband twice.

Hat: Cut out as for other Hat.

Sewing: Dungarees: Press under the seam allowances of the pockets all around and top-stitch 1.5 cm (⅝") from the upper edges. Stitch 2 pockets to the back where marked, working close to the edge. Join the outer leg seams to the arrows. At this point, snip diagonally into the seam allowance of the back pants section. Turn in the self-facings of the front and back on the fold line. Join inner leg seams, then crotch seam, and center back. Join the center back facing seam, then stitch facing to pants back. Turn and top-stitch the edges. Bib and waistband are worked double: Stitch 1 bib to each waistband. Then stitch both bib/waistband pieces together and turn, leaving the waist seam open (point p). Stitch a single layer of the waistband to the pants front, right sides facing. Turn under the seam allowance of the inside layer and stitch down from the outside along the seamline. Stitch the pocket to the bib where marked. Turn the hem under twice and stitch. Make buttonholes, sew on buttons and attach buckles.

Hat: Work as for other Hat.

1726

Tough kids

Style 1

Style 2

Some enchanted evening

The style and cut of these lovely dresses is simple — it's the fabric that tells the story — so don't skimp on the quality or the cost. Then you'll shine, no matter how elegant or formal the occasion.

Style 1: This demure but elegant dress can be made in sizes D and F from Pattern Sheet 54. Shown here in crêpe de chine, it has a flattering, low-cut neckline. The Empire line is accentuated by a narrow band which extends into ties at the back and the full-cut sleeves are gathered into deep cuffs with looped buttonings. The two unpressed pleats of the skirt create a flowing width.

Style 2: This second style is cunning and stunning in its simplicity. You can make it in sizes B and D from Pattern Sheet 54. The top is made from sequined fabric and the skirt falls from the waist in sunray pleats.

Style 2

Illustrated Sewing
54

Style 3

This third version can also be made from Pattern Sheet 54 in sizes B and D. The lace used to make the bodice has a scalloped edge which has been used to trim the waist and sleeves. The round-necked bodice is lined throughout, while the sleeves are transparent. The skirt is full and pleated.

Cutting and stitching lace

Machine-made lace is widely available for dressmaking in many qualities, weights, and designs. The lighter weights of lace are the easiest to use because they can be sewn in the same way as any other fabric. However, you should allow plenty of time for laying out and cutting out the pattern pieces. Arrange the pattern pieces so that the design of the lace is used in the most effective way and the motifs match along the seamlines. The lace can be cut without it fraying as long as you cut around the motifs and not through them. If a style is lined, baste the lace and lining together and treat them as a single layer of fabric. Finish the raw edges together and when inserting the zipper, sew it in by hand.

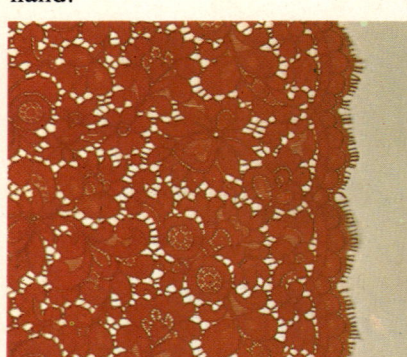

1 The photograph above shows a sample of lace. Instead of a straight selvage, there is a scalloped edge on one or both sides. This edge can be used decoratively on the hem or other edges. If used in this way, you can cut out the piece crosswise on the lace because it has no grain. Always cut out from a single layer of fabric and transfer all markings and seamlines with basting or tailor's chalk.

How-to

2 The seams of lightweight lace are stitched as for any other fabric. Finish them with close zigzag stitching just beyond the stitching line, and then cut away the excess seam allowance. Do not cut through the stitching line.

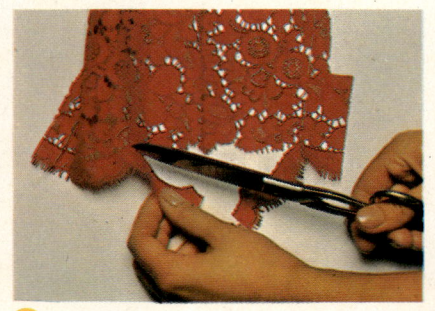

3 To retain scallops on a hem or sleeve without losing the curved shape, cut the piece so that the scallops lie on the hemline at the deepest part of the curve; the rest extends. Stitch seam to just above edging, then cut off edging.

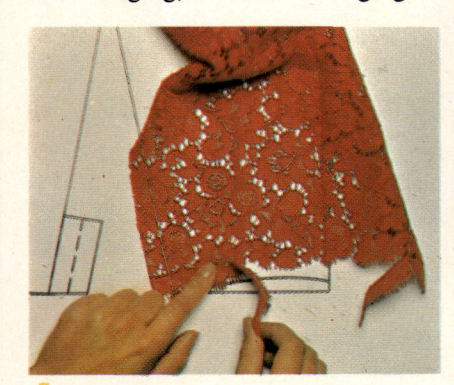

4 Place the lace sleeve on your pattern piece, then reshape the edge along the marked line with the lace edging. Clip between scallops to make it lie flat.

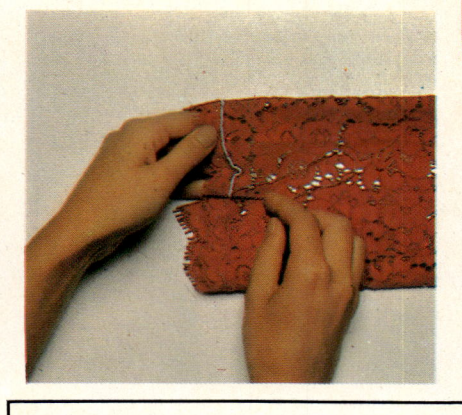

5 Baste the scalloped edge firmly in place. Appliqué the edging to the piece with small overcasting stitches. Sew with doubled thread in a matching color so that the stitches are secure, but invisible. Cut away the excess lace under the edging, close to the stitching.

Stitching permanently pleated fabric

The pleats of permanently pleated fabrics have been pressed in by machine. There are two types of pleating – straight and sunray.

Straight pleating, as the name implies, has pleats of equal width from waist to hem.

Sunray pleats are wider at the hem than at the waist edge, so the longer the skirt, the wider the pleats at the hem. This type of fabric is pleated in half or quarter circles and for a full, swinging skirt, you will require a full circle of fabric. We have used this latter type of fabric for these dresses.

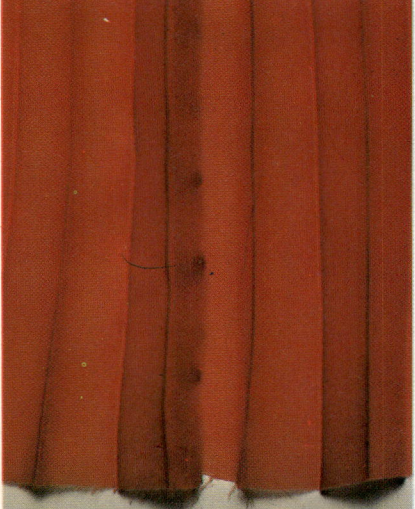

1 Make all seams along the inside fold of a pleat. When using sunray pleating, begin basting at the waist to ensure that you will have enough seam allowance. Stitch the pleat, then finish the allowances together and press them to one side.

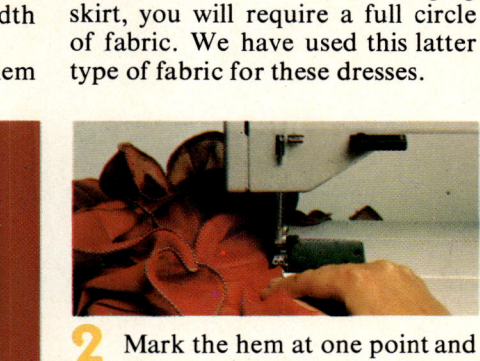

2 Mark the hem at one point and then hang the skirt on a dressmaking form or on a hanger. Mark the correct length all the way around the skirt. Turn under the hem and baste in place. Stitch over the fold line with small zigzag stitches as shown. Trim away the excess at hem, close to stitching.

3 To distribute the pleats evenly around the waist, pull the pleats so that the fabric lies flat. Baste edge with long stitches, then gather to the required width.

Illustrated Sewing 55

Take your choice

Shirts are an essential part of any daytime wardrobe because they can be teamed with skirts and pants of any style. Four variations of the classic shirt are given on Pattern Sheet 55.

Style 1: The checked fabric here makes the style casual and sporting. It is hip length and has a button band down the front. The bias-cut shoulder yoke is extended and inserted into the top of the full sleeve (see the photograph above). This shirt is made in one size to fit sizes A to C. If made for the smaller size, it will fit loosely; for the larger size it will be close fitting.

Style 1

Style 2

Style 3

Style 2: This smart striped shirt is in sizes D and F on the pattern sheet; sizes C, E, and G can also be adapted. The fabric has been chosen for its slimming effect, but some care needs to be taken to match the diagonal stripes when cutting out. This style has an open collar and standard shirt sleeves and cuffs. It is equally effective when made up in cool cotton or warm wool. It's your choice.

Style 3: Here, the shirt shape is the same as Style 2, but we've added a small patch pocket on the left front, a yoke at the back, and a fuller sleeve gathered into a cuff. This style is also in sizes D and F.

Now we're up to three and there's one style more — see overleaf.

How-to

Inserting an extended yoke

The photograph above shows the pattern pieces, laid out and ready for assembly. The seamlines have been marked and the seam allowances have been finished. The back is at the top of the photograph, the sleeve is on the right, the front is at the bottom, and the yoke is in the center. The cross marks on the yoke divide it into two sections. The longer section is sewn to the front and back, while the shorter section is inserted into the sleeve.

1 Gather the top edges of the front and back to the length indicated on the pattern, then stitch the side and sleeve seams. Set in the sleeves, stitching from one yoke seam to the other. Finish the armhole seam allowances together and press them toward the sleeve.

2 Stitch the end of the yoke to the sleeve, right sides facing. Stitch with the garment side up and the yoke underneath. Stitch exactly into the corners and fasten the threads securely. Note: For clarity, the photograph shows this stage from the other side.

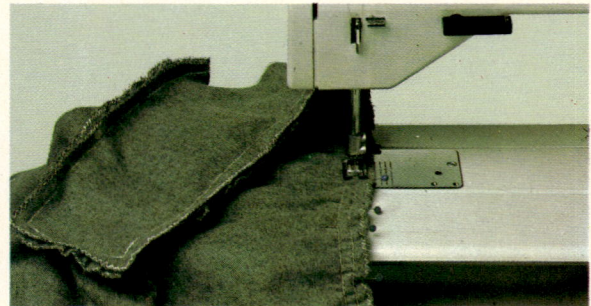

3 Clip diagonally into the seam allowance at the corner, clipping close to the stitching line. Stitch the yoke to the front and back with the gathered side up and the yoke underneath. This will make it easier to stitch the gathers.

4 Draw out the basting threads from below the yoke seam. Press the seam allowances toward the yoke and baste in place. Finally, top-stitch all around, 0.75 cm ($\frac{3}{4}$″) from the seam.

Style 4: This shirt is made from the same pattern as Style 1, and the difference is in the detailing. The front band is open and does not continue the full length of the front; it is inserted and finished with decorative top-stitching. Again, the shoulder yoke is extended into the sleeve with top-stitching to match the front band. The stand-up collar matches the cuffs.

Style 4

Illustrated Sewing 56

Family tartans

This family is starting off the day in the smartest possible way, with warm dressing gowns in traditional tartan. All three styles wrap snugly around and are secured with a tie belt.

Style 1: First, a dressing gown given in sizes V and X. It is mid-calf length and cut straight. Buttoned down the front, it has a small, neat collar. Use a brightly-colored tartan to cheer her up on the dullest of mornings. Then she can slip her arms into the wide, full sleeves, tuck her hands into large patch pockets, and wrap up to be as warm as toast!

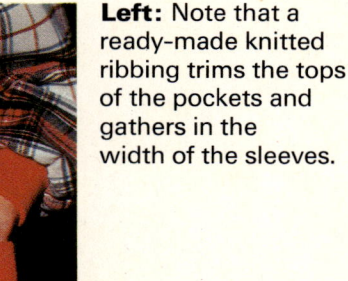

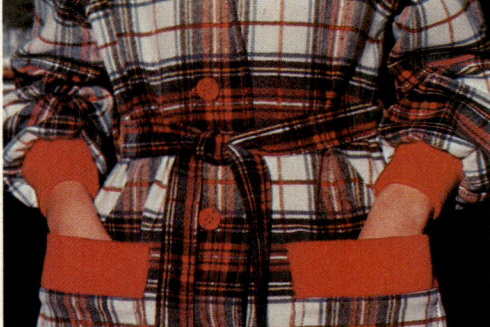

Left: Note that a ready-made knitted ribbing trims the tops of the pockets and gathers in the width of the sleeves.

Style 2: The woman's dressing gown is in sizes C and E. The style is to the floor and buttoned up the front. The front and back are gathered onto yokes, which are bias-cut. The sleeves are straight and full, but here the length is turned back in deep cuffs. Bias-cut pockets with deep flaps repeat the theme, and a tie belt, stitched to the back as far as the side seams, holds everything together neatly. Why not make it today!

Style 3: We haven't forgotten the man of the house. This dressing gown is in sizes M and O. We've incorporated several design features to please him such as its straight-cut, the mid-calf length, the large collar, and three patch pockets. The sleeves are wide, with no cuffs. Because it has no fastenings, it will fit a large or a slim figure. The classic design also makes it suitable for fabrics other than a tartan. Try it in towelling to wear after a bath or in rich silk for a luxury look.

Making a shawl collar

On the pattern sheet you will find the pattern pieces for the bias-cut under collar and the upper collar with a cut-in-one front facing. Interface the two halves of the under collar with iron-on interfacing and the front facing edges with non-iron-on interfacing. The upper collar is larger than the under collar so that the collar will roll well. You may have to vary this additional width, depending on the thickness of the fabric used.

1 Iron the interfacings to the two halves of the under collar, then stitch the center back seam. Stitch the non-iron-on interfacing onto the front seam allowance, close to the marked seamline. Stitch the shoulder seams, then stitch the under collar around the neck edge, right sides facing. Stitch from the front edge into the corner on both fronts, catching in the interfacing as you do so. Fasten off securely. Clip diagonally into the seam allowance at the corners. Stitch the collar around the neck. Press open seams from front edge to corner; around neck, press seam allowances toward collar.

How-to

2. Cut away the seam allowances at the corners as shown above.

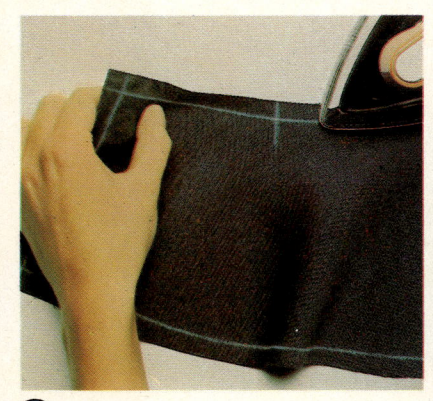

3. With a steam iron or a damp cloth, stretch the upper collar where marked on the pattern piece. Stitch the center back seam and finish the inside edge.

4. Stitch the upper collar, right sides facing, along the marked line on the outside edge. Stitch the facings to the front edges and upper collar to under collar.

5. Turn the upper collar to the right side. Baste the outside (seam) edge carefully with diagonal basting stitches so that the seam is not visible from the right side. Top-stitch the collar.

6. Baste the remaining open edge of the upper collar along the seam of the under collar around the neck edge, then stitch into the seam through all layers. If you have used a fabric other than a medium-weight wool, you may need to trim the under collar seam allowance at this point to reduce the bulk around neck. Finish neck edge seam allowance with zigzag stitching. The completed collar is shown in the large photograph.

Togged out for town or country

Choose full-length or knee-length pants. The pattern is given in sizes U and W on Pattern Sheet 56.

STYLE 1

Materials Required: Woollen fabric, 150 cm (60") wide: 0.90 m (1 yd) for size U; 1 m (1⅛ yds) for size W.
Zipper: 14 cm (6") long. 1 button. Iron-on interfacing for the waistband.

Cutting out: The cutting layout is shown below. Seam allowances: hem, 4 cm (1½"); side seams, 2 cm (¾"); elsewhere, 1 cm (⅜"). Waistband: cut 1 strip 6 cm (2¼") wide and 63 cm (24¾") or 65 cm (25⅝") long (of which 2 cm (¾") is underlap), plus 1 cm (⅜") seam allowance.

Sewing: Stitch the pocket lining to the front pocket opening, right sides facing. Turn and top-stitch. Place the pocket back under the pocket lining, right sides facing. Join the pocket parts and finish the seam allowances together. Now stitch the back hip yokes onto the backs, right sides facing. Finish the seam allowances together, press toward the yokes, and top-stitch the yokes. Join the side seams, then the inner leg seams and finish. Turn up the hem. Press in creases. Join the crotch seam up to the zipper. For the zipper, see the diagram. At the overlap, press under the self-facing along the center front line. At the underlap, push the facing out about 0.5 cm (¼") and press. Press the separate underlap piece along the fold line, wrong sides facing. Place the right-hand zipper tape onto the underlap so that the tape edge lines up with the cut edges; stitch all edges together with zigzag stitching. Place the separate underlap piece (with the stitched-on zipper half) just underneath the right-hand pressed edge of the zipper opening. Now stitch through all layers. Close the zipper. Place the left-hand edge of the zipper opening over the zipper so that it is fully covered. Pin the zipper in place on the facing only. Stitch once beside the zipper teeth and once at the tape edge. Then fold the facing under and stitch from the right side of the pants along the marked line.
Iron the interfacing onto the waistband, stitch it on, and top-stitch all around. Make a buttonhole in the waistband and sew on the button.

STYLE 2

Materials Required: You will need about 3 suede skins. However, take the pattern with you when buying the suede as skins vary in size.
Zipper: 14 cm (6") long. 3 buttons. Leather needle for sewing machine.

Cutting out: Trace the pattern outlines onto the back of the skin with a ball-point pen. On the following seams, add no allowances: on inner and side leg seams of pants fronts, on back pants seam of hip yoke, at slanting edge of pocket. Elsewhere, add 1 cm (⅜") seam allowance. Slit facings: cut out twice with the crossed area, twice without, each with 1 cm (⅜") seam allowance on one short end. Waistband: cut a strip 3 cm (1¼") wide and 64 cm (25¼") long or 68 cm (26¾") long (of which 2 cm (¾") is underlap and 1 cm (⅜") is seam allowance of overlap).

Sewing: Turn the seam allowance of the front pocket opening over the cut edge of the pocket lining and stitch. (Don't pin the seams; hold together with adhesive tape). Place the pocket back under the pocket lining, right sides facing. Join the pocket. Now stitch the hip yokes, wrong side over right side, onto the seam allowance of the backs, once close to the edge and again at presser foot width from edge. Join side seams down to slit, placing the fronts over seam allowance of backs. Stitch the slit facing (without cross) onto seam allowance of back to form underlap. Stitch facing with cross, wrong side onto right side, onto the front, lining up the outer edges. Stitch the decorative cross. Now join inner leg seams in same way as side seams. Form pleats as shown on pattern and stitch along seam allowance. Stitch kneeband, wrong side onto right side of leg seam allowance and top-stitch all around. Join crotch seam, right sides facing, to beginning of zipper. Fold the seam allowance toward the zipper overlap and top-stitch. Sew in zipper as for Style 1. Stitch on waistband, wrong side onto right side seam allowance, turning in 1 cm (⅜") of overlap. Top-stitch. Make buttonholes, stitching a scrap underneath. Sew on buttons.

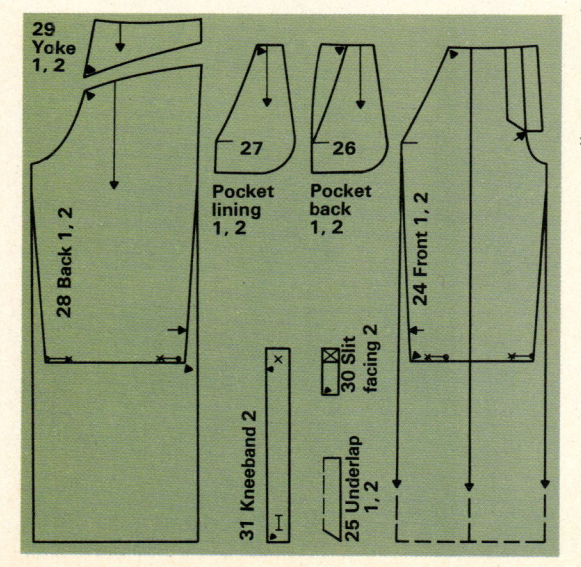

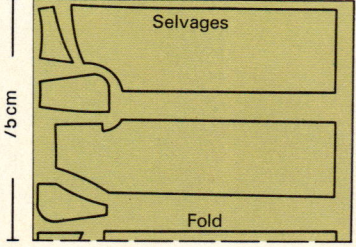

Left: These pattern pieces are given actual size on Pattern Sheet 56. The knee-length legs are shown inside the full-length legs.
Above: The cutting layout for Style 1.
Right: Inserting the zipper into the pants.

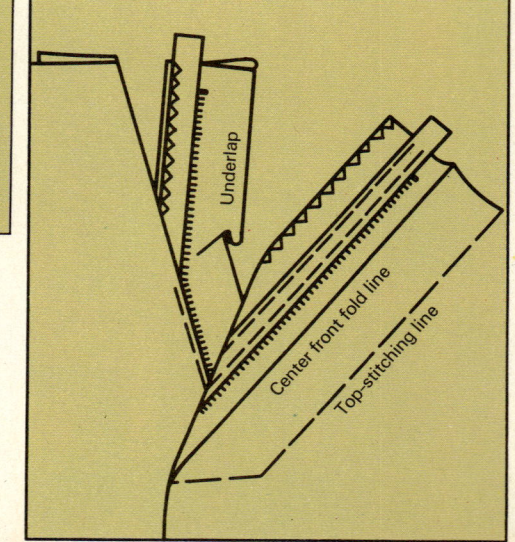

◀ The cut of these pants ensures a perfect fit. The long pants (Style 1) are made in a woollen fabric, the knee-length pants (Style 2) in suede. Both are from the same pattern.

The kneeband draws in the width of the legs and is fastened at the side with a button.

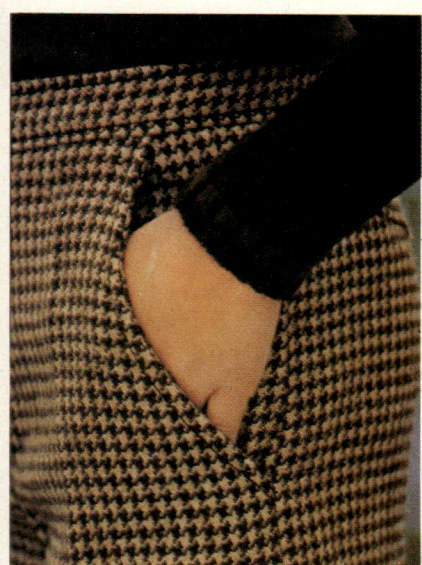

The slanted pocket opening, shown here on the long pants, is the same for both of the styles.

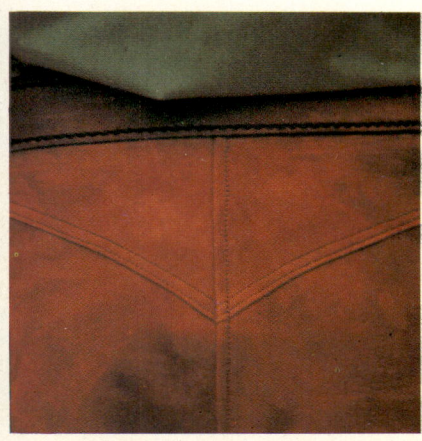

Both pants have a hip yoke below the back waistband to give a good fit, as shown here on the knee-length style.

1741

Divided attention

Culottes are practical garments for a little girl because they allow freedom of movement, yet look smart enough for most occasions. Our easy-to-sew version is in printed corduroy.

Size: Size V: 61 cm (24") waist, 72 cm (28½") hips; Size X: 63 cm (24¾") waist, 76 cm (29¾") hips. Sizes U, W, and Y can also be adapted.

Materials Required: Printed corduroy: 1.45 m (1⅝ yds), 90 cm (36") wide for Size V; 1.50 m (1¾ yds), 90 cm (36") wide for Size X. Remnant of lining fabric for the pockets. Iron-on woven interfacing: 0.10 m (⅛ yd), 90 cm (36") wide. Zipper: 14 cm (6") long. 1 button.

Cutting out: The actual-size pattern pieces are given on Pattern Sheet 55. For hints about cutting out corduroy, see Pattern Sheet 25. Cut out the pieces from single fabric.

Seam allowances: add 4 cm (1½") for the hem, 1.5 cm (⅝") elsewhere.

Cut out the pocket twice in lining. For the waistband, cut a strip 7 cm (2¾") wide and 64 cm or 66 cm (25¼" or 26") long (of which 2 cm (¾") is underlap) plus seam allowance. Cut out the waistband in interfacing and iron on.

Sewing: Stitch the back hip yoke onto the skirt back. Finish seam allowance, press upward, and top-stitch 0.75 cm (¼") from the seam. Fold over the top of the back pockets and stitch down at the pocket sides. Press under the seam allowances. Stitch the decorative cross as shown on the pattern. Stitch on the back pockets close to the edge and again 0.75 cm (¼") away.

Stitch the pocket lining to the pocket opening of the skirt front, right sides facing, turn and top-stitch 0.75 cm (¼") from the edge. Place pocket back under skirt front where marked and join pocket pieces. Join skirt side seams, catching in pocket. Join the inner leg seams. Press the seam allowances open and finish them. Join the crotch seam up to the zipper mark.

Press under the facing on the right-hand side of the zipper opening along the marked line

The culottes have a back hip yoke and two patch pockets. The front view on the right shows the side pockets and the zipper fastening. All seams are finished with top-stitching.

(i.e. center front); on the left-hand side, press it 1 cm ($\frac{3}{8}$") beyond the line. Place the left half of the zipper close under the left-hand edge and stitch close to the fold. Close the zipper. Place the right-hand side over the zipper so that the center front lines are over one another, then stitch down along the marked line.

Stitch on the waistband with a 2 cm ($\frac{3}{4}$") underlap, catching in the pockets at the upper edge. Top-stitch all around 0.75 cm ($\frac{1}{4}$") from the edge.

Work a buttonhole into the waistband and sew on the button. Press under the hem and stitch 3 cm ($1\frac{1}{4}$") from the edge.

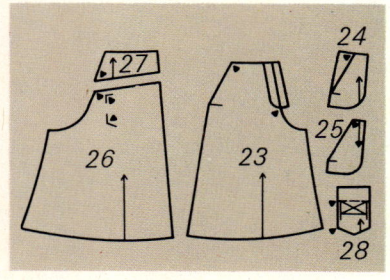

Above: The pattern pieces which are given actual size on Pattern Sheet 55.
Below: The cutting layout.

The dungarees on the left are made in a flowered cotton. They have a zipper, a belt casing at the waist, and patch pockets. The dungarees on the right are made from the same pattern, but in a tough, striped cotton.

For work and play

Everyday clothes for children should be practical, but they certainly need not be boring. These dungarees and jackets for girls or boys are bright, stylish, and easy-care.

Size: 62 cm (24¼") chest, 68 cm (26¾") hips.

DUNGAREES

Materials Required: Flowered or striped cotton: 2.25 m (2½ yds), 90 cm (36") wide. Unfolded bias binding: 2.20 m (2⅜ yds), 2.5 cm (1") wide. Zipper: 30 cm (12") long. Elastic: 0.50 m (⅝ yd), 3 cm (1¼") wide. One button.

Cutting out: Seam allowances: 2 cm (¾") at leg and shoulder seams; 2 cm (¾") at front zipper edge; 1 cm (⅜") at crotch seam, increasing to 2 cm (¾") at center back seam; 0.5 cm (¼") at neck edge; 4 cm (1½") at hem; 1 cm (⅜") elsewhere. Cut out dungarees in single fabric. Cut the tab twice and the casing once on the fold. Cut the patch pocket twice.

Sewing: Finish all cut edges other than at neck edges. Join shoulder seams. Place bias binding along neck edges, right sides facing. Stitch 0.5 cm (¼") in from edges, turn to inside, turn under 0.5 cm (¼") and stitch. Join side seams and inside leg seams. Join center back seam, continuing along the crotch seam up to front zipper opening. Turn in seam allowance of the zipper opening and stitch in zipper. Press under the casing seam allowance and stitch on along the long sides. Stitch and turn tabs, make a buttonhole in one of them and stitch them to the ends of the 50 cm (19½") elastic. Draw this through the casing and stitch across the openings through all layers. Miter the corners of the pocket and press under seam allowances all around. Stitch on pockets with openings at sides. Stitch hem. Sew button onto tab.

JACKET

Materials Required: Denim: 2.20 m (2⅜ yds), 90 cm (36") wide. Bias binding: 3.30 m (3⅝ yds), 2 cm (¾") wide. Zipper: 18 cm (7") long. Elastic: 0.40 m (½ yd), 3 cm (1¼") wide. 1 button.

Cutting out: Seam allowances: Add no seam allowances on edges to be bound; add 4 cm (1½") to sleeve hem; 2 cm (¾") to sleeve seam, side seam, and front seam; elsewhere add 1 cm (⅜"). Cut out in double fabric. The front has a center front seam to make it easier to work the slit. Cut out patch pocket and flap once each; cut underarm gusset twice on the bias.

Sewing: Finish all cut edges other than those to be bound. Join center front seam from hem to arrow. Join shoulder seams and side seams where indicated. Join upper center seam of hood, then the crosswise seam. Form pleats by placing X onto O and stitch along seam allowance. Stitch hood to neck edge, right sides facing. Bind hood and slit with the bias binding. Bind hem edge and side slit in the same way. Stitch in the zipper. Bind pocket and flap; do not bind the flap top edge.

Stitch on pocket where indicated. Work buttonhole into flap and stitch on 1 cm (⅜") above the pocket, right sides facing. Turn down flap, top-stitch close to top edge. Sew button onto pocket. Join sleeve seam between beginning of gusset and hem allowance at wrist. Turn in the sleeve hem allowance and stitch down close to upper edge. Draw a wrist length of elastic through sleeve hem. Set in sleeve where marked. Press seam allowances of gusset to inside, then baste it on where indicated and stitch from the right side, close to the edge.

The two jackets are also made from the same pattern, one in blue, the other in scarlet denim. Both have hoods, a large patch pocket, and side slits. The wrists are elasticized; the edges are bound with contrasting-colored bias binding.

Draw pattern pieces to the measurements given. The numbers are centimeters; inch equivalents are given below.

Inch equivalents:

1 cm	= 3/8″	10 cm	= 3 7/8″
1.5 cm	= 3/4″	11 cm	= 4 3/8″
2 cm	= 7/8″	13 cm	= 5 1/8″
2.5 cm	= 1″	14 cm	= 5 5/8″
3 cm	= 1 1/8″	15 cm	= 5 7/8″
3.5 cm	= 1 3/8″	16 cm	= 6 1/4″
4 cm	= 1 5/8″	16.5 cm	= 6 1/2″
4.5 cm	= 1 7/8″	17 cm	= 6 3/4″
5 cm	= 2″	18 cm	= 7 1/8″
5.5 cm	= 2 1/2″	19 cm	= 7 1/2″
6 cm	= 2 3/8″	20 cm	= 7 7/8″
6.2 cm	= 2 3/8″	21 cm	= 8 1/4″
6.5 cm	= 2 1/2″	25 cm	= 9 7/8″
7 cm	= 2 3/4″	27 cm	= 10 5/8″
7.5 cm	= 3″	28 cm	= 11″
8 cm	= 3 1/8″	30 cm	= 11 3/4″
8.5 cm	= 3 3/8″	31 cm	= 12 1/4″
9 cm	= 3 1/2″	36 cm	= 14 1/8″
9.3 cm	= 3 5/8″	50 cm	= 19 5/8″
9.5 cm	= 3 3/4″	51 cm	= 20 1/8″

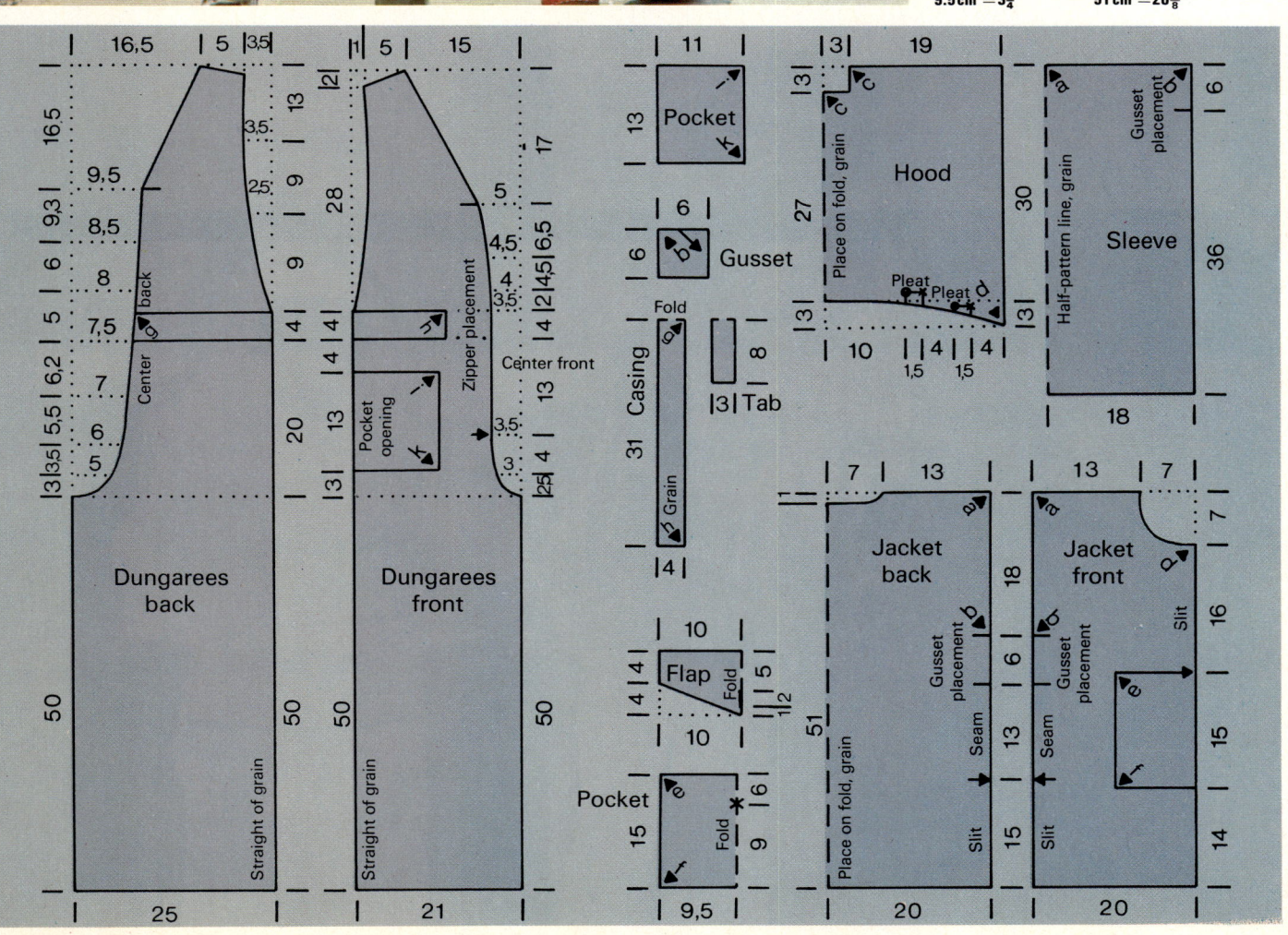

1745

A touch of jean-ius

◄ Here, a pair of flared jeans was used. For the bag, cut off the jeans at crotch level. Make the carrying straps from the upper leg fabric and thread two bamboo sticks through the belt loops to hold the top rigid. From the lower leg parts, you can make a child's skirt on the same principle as the straight skirt. ▼

▲ Transform an old pair of jeans into a skirt and hat. For the skirt, just cut off the legs to the desired length, remove the inside leg seam stitching, and join again as front and back center seams. Work a slit at the back with loop fastenings. The hat is made from the remnants. ►

1746

Old jeans never die — they can live on forever in different guises. If you have a pair which is worn thin in places, make use of the rest of the fabric to sew a new denim outfit. Here are plenty of ideas for some clever recycling.

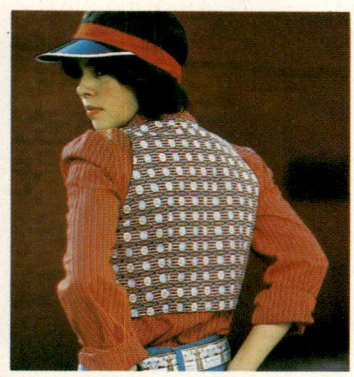

◀ The Bermuda shorts are made from a pair of flared jeans which were tight at the knees. The shorts are cut off at knee level and a side slit is made. From the lower legs, you can make the front parts of the bolero. Just buy a piece of suitable fabric for the bolero back and lining.

▲ As a variation, you can make a child's bib skirt. The bib is made from a back leg and pocket and the little skirt is cut from the lower leg parts.

1747

Straight skirt and hat
These are made from a pair of straight-cut jeans.

Skirt: Remove the crotch seam stitching at the front to just below the zipper opening, at the back to the yoke seam. Remove the inside leg seams and pin the front and back legs over one another so that the center seam runs straight. Then try on the skirt. You may find that removing the crotch seam causes wrinkles at the back waist. If this happens, remove the waistband seam to about the side seam and push the surplus width into the waistband. Join the center seams, leaving a 25 cm (10") slit at the lower back, trim off the seam allowance to 1 cm ($\frac{3}{8}$"), and finish cut edges. Stitch the hem. Make 7 loops for the slit fastening and baste under at left edge of slit. Top-stitch slit, catching in the loops. Cover 7 buttons with denim and sew on to correspond to loops.

Hat: $\frac{1}{2}$ of the crown and brim sections are given actual size. Draw the whole of each section onto tissue paper and cut out 4 times each. Iron interfacing onto all the sections, stitch the crown parts together, right sides facing and top-stitch on both sides of the seams. The brim is made double and has a seam at front and back. Stitch along outer edge and turn, then stitch the crown onto the brim, close to the edge. Punch eyelets into crown if desired.

Bag and child's skirt
These are from jeans with tight knees and flared legs.

Bag: You will need 2 bamboo sticks and each 40 cm (16") long and 2 toggles. Cut off the legs at the end of the front crotch seam and sew the jeans together in a slight curve toward the sides. Finish edges. Stitch up the zipper opening. Make straps from the upper legs of the jeans, cutting 2 strips each 6 cm ($2\frac{1}{2}$") wide and 50 cm ($19\frac{1}{2}$") long. Press 1 cm ($\frac{3}{8}$") to the inside at long sides, then fold the pressed edges in to the center to make straps 2 cm ($\frac{3}{4}$") wide. Stitch close to pressed edges through all layers. Turn the ends in 4 cm ($1\frac{1}{2}$") and stitch them on beside the belt loops at waistband. On the front pockets, fasten a loop and a toggle, stitching the loop under at the pocket edge with the toggle to correspond. Then draw the bamboo sticks through the belt loops.

Child's skirt: You can make this skirt for any age, cutting it as long as the width of the legs will allow. Use one leg for each side of the skirt. Cut off the legs at the required height and remove the inside leg seam stitching and the hem. Leave the outside leg seams joined. Rejoin the inside leg seams to form front and back skirt seams and finish edges. Leave an opening at the back for a 16 cm (6") zipper. Stitch a piece of bias binding to waist, right sides facing, turn to inside and top-stitch the edges. Even up the skirt hem, turn up, and stitch. Make belt loops and stitch on at waist.

Bermuda shorts with bolero, child's bib skirt
These are from jeans with tight knees and flared legs.

Bermuda shorts: Cut off the jeans above the knee and make a slit in the outside leg seam at each side.

Bolero: The pattern pieces are shown on the diagram. The measurements given will fit an 80 cm ($31\frac{1}{2}$") chest. The fronts are cut from the remnants of the legs. Buy a suitable fabric for the back and for the lining. Stitch, turn and top-stitch the flaps. Join front yoke seams, catching in flaps, and top-stitch. Make darts at the back, then join the side seams. Make the lining in the same way. Stitch and turn the bolero and lining and top-stitch close to the edge. Cover buttons with the jeans fabric and stitch over the flaps to fasten them down.

Bib skirt: Make the front and back of skirt as described for the other child's skirt. The bib is made from a back pocket. Cut out with about 3 cm (1") extra at top and sides and 2 cm ($\frac{3}{4}$") at base. For the shoulder straps, check the length with strips of muslin first, then cut 2 strips 6 cm ($2\frac{1}{2}$") wide.

The waistband length depends on the waist measurement. Cut 2 strips 6 cm ($2\frac{1}{2}$") wide by waist length plus 3 cm (1") underlap. Stitch and turn the straps and punch 3 press stud uppers into each, 3.5 cm ($1\frac{1}{2}$") apart. Press 1 cm ($\frac{3}{8}$") under at top and sides of bib and stitch down. Punch a press stud bottom into each side of bib, 1 cm ($\frac{3}{8}$") from top. Stitch the waistband along the short sides and the top edge, catching in the bib at the front and the shoulder straps about 3 cm (1") from the center back (with a slight diagonal slant to prevent them slipping off the shoulders). Turn waistband to right side.

Stitch one layer of waistband to the skirt, right sides facing. Press seam allowance upward. Turn under the allowance on inner layer and stitch down along the seam from the right side. Punch a press stud into the waistband at back.

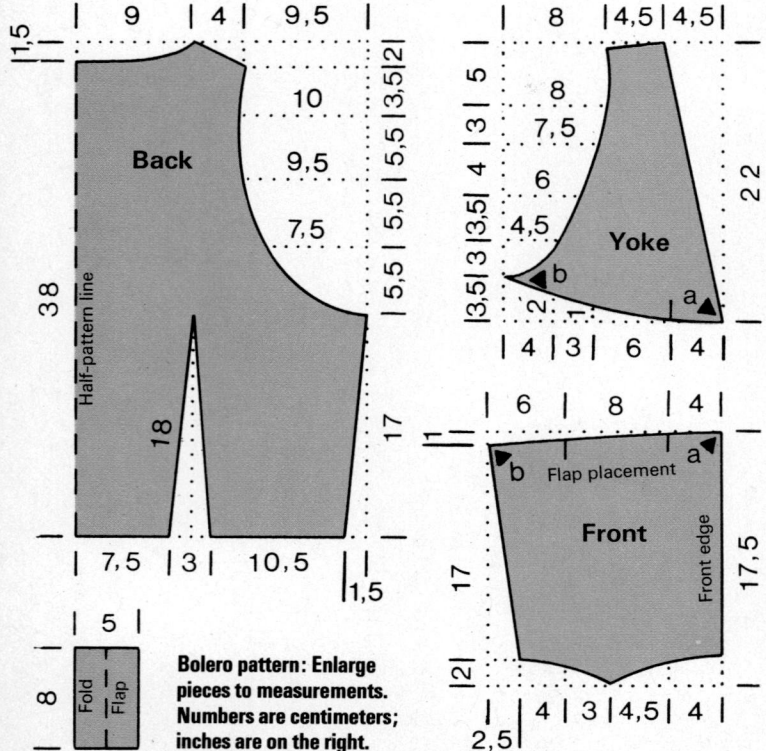

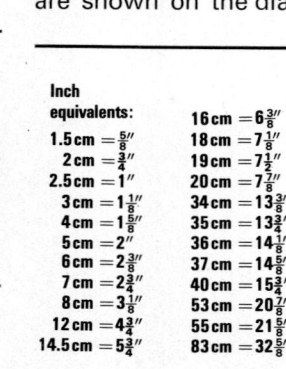

Bolero pattern: Enlarge pieces to measurements. Numbers are centimeters; inches are on the right.

Inch equivalents:	
1.5 cm = $\frac{5}{8}$"	16 cm = $6\frac{3}{8}$"
2 cm = $\frac{3}{4}$"	18 cm = $7\frac{1}{4}$"
2.5 cm = 1"	19 cm = $7\frac{1}{2}$"
3 cm = $1\frac{1}{8}$"	20 cm = $7\frac{7}{8}$"
4 cm = $1\frac{5}{8}$"	34 cm = $13\frac{3}{8}$"
5 cm = 2"	35 cm = $13\frac{3}{4}$"
6 cm = $2\frac{3}{8}$"	36 cm = $14\frac{1}{8}$"
7 cm = $2\frac{3}{4}$"	37 cm = $14\frac{5}{8}$"
8 cm = $3\frac{1}{8}$"	40 cm = $15\frac{3}{4}$"
12 cm = $4\frac{3}{4}$"	53 cm = $20\frac{7}{8}$"
14.5 cm = $5\frac{3}{4}$"	55 cm = $21\frac{5}{8}$"
	83 cm = $32\frac{5}{8}$"

Double duffle

Sports kit, weekend gear, even your shopping will pack away easily into this stylish duffle bag.

Materials Required:

Striped bag: Deck chair canvas: 1.60 m (1¾ yd), 45 cm (18") wide.

Plain bag: Sailcloth: 0.65 m (¾ yd), 90 cm (36") wide. Leather for base and lower strip (place seams according to size of skin).

Both bags: Zipper 20 cm (8") long. 12 eyelets (medium size). About 2 m (2¼ yds) of cord. 1 small-snap swivel hook.

Cutting out: Both bags: Cut out the parts given in the diagram once each. The main part has 2 cm (¾") seam allowance at upper edge, elsewhere add 1 cm (⅜").
For the loop fastening for the hook on both bags, cut a strip 8 cm (3") long, adjusting the width according to size of hook.

Plain bag: Cut out the leather parts with ½ cm (¼") seam allowance.

Sewing: Both bags: Turn under the seam allowance of the patch pocket at sides and zipper edge. Stitch zipper under, visibly on the plain bag, covered on the striped bag. Fold under seam allowances at top and bottom edges and stitch on pocket. Punch in the eyelets where marked.

Striped bag: Join one side seam of the main part. Stitch lower strip to the main part. Join second side seam.

Both bags: Stitch on base with right sides facing on striped bag, with wrong sides facing on plain bag. Catch in the strip for the hook at center back. Turn in the seam allowance at upper edge and stitch down. Draw the cord through the eyelets from center front to center back, through the hook at the base, and back to center front. Knot the ends separately here.

Enlarge the pattern pieces to actual size from the diagram. Measurements are in cm (inch equivalents are also given). Draw a circle with a 12 cm (4¾") radius for base.

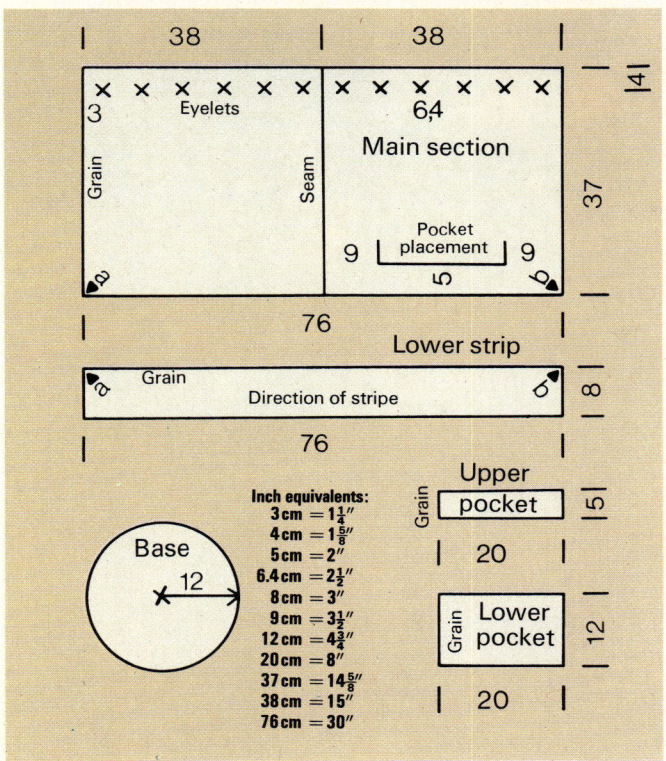

Inch equivalents:
3 cm = 1⅛"
4 cm = 1⅝"
5 cm = 2"
6.4 cm = 2½"
8 cm = 3"
9 cm = 3½"
12 cm = 4¾"
20 cm = 8"
37 cm = 14⅝"
38 cm = 15"
76 cm = 30"

The striped bag (top) is made of deck chair canvas, while the plain bag is made of sailcloth trimmed with a leather base.

1749

The happy wanderer

Our nylon version is waterproof with padded straps and press stud fastenings.

Materials Required:

Nylon back pack: Nylon fabric: 0.70m ($\frac{3}{4}$ yd), 115 cm (45") wide. Nylon tape: 2.80m (3$\frac{1}{8}$ yds), 5 cm (2") wide. Nylon cord: 1.20m (1$\frac{3}{8}$ yds), 3mm ($\frac{1}{8}$") thick. 18 eyelets. 10 medium press studs. 2 swivel hooks (about 6 cm (2$\frac{1}{2}$") long) and 4 matching rings. 2 strips of foam rubber each 4cm (1$\frac{1}{2}$") wide and 50cm (19$\frac{1}{2}$") long. Firm fabric as interfacing to reinforce studs and eyelets. Canvas back pack: Canvas: 1.50 m (1$\frac{5}{8}$ yds), 90 cm (36") wide. Strong webbing: 2.80m (3$\frac{1}{8}$ yds), 6 cm (2$\frac{1}{2}$") wide. Cotton cord: 3.70 m (4 yds), 3 mm ($\frac{1}{8}$") thick. 32 eyelets. 2 swivel hooks (about 6 cm (2$\frac{1}{2}$") long) and 4 matching rings. 2 strips of foam rubber, each 5 cm (2") wide and 50 cm (19$\frac{1}{2}$") long. Iron-on interfacing.

Cutting out: Cut out back with 2 cm ($\frac{3}{4}$") added all around, but leave flap without seam allowance. Cut out front and patch pocket with 5 cm (2") seam allowance at upper edge and 2 cm ($\frac{3}{4}$") elsewhere. Cut out pocket flap twice in fabric and once in interfacing with 1 cm ($\frac{3}{8}$") seam allowance. For the shoulder straps, cut 2 nylon or webbing bands, each 1 m (39$\frac{1}{2}$") long. From nylon tape or canvas, cut 1 strip 5 cm (2") wide and 14 cm (5$\frac{1}{2}$") long and 2 strips each 5 cm (2") wide and 18 cm (7") long.

Sewing: Both packs: Reinforce seam allowance at upper front edge with interfacing, finish raw edge, turn seam allowance to inside and stitch down. Repeat with patch pocket. Cut 2 strips of interfacing 4 cm (1$\frac{5}{8}$") wide and 14 cm (5$\frac{1}{2}$") long and reinforce either side of front, 3 cm (1$\frac{1}{8}$") from upper edge and along the tuck line. Punch in eyelets along top edge, placing 4 on each side and 10 on front, 1.5 cm ($\frac{5}{8}$") away from edge.

Canvas back pack: On either side of front, punch in 4 eyelets in a vertical line. Place them 2 cm ($\frac{3}{4}$") apart, beginning 5 cm (2") from top edge and 2 cm ($\frac{3}{4}$") from tuck.

Both packs: Reinforce one pocket flap, then stitch pocket flap, right sides together, leaving upper edge open. Turn and topstitch. Finish raw edges together.

Nylon back pack: Punch the top of 1 press stud into each corner of pocket flap and 2 lower studs into each corner of pocket (for adjusting).

Canvas back pack: On each side of patch pocket, punch in 2 eyelets, 5 cm (2") from

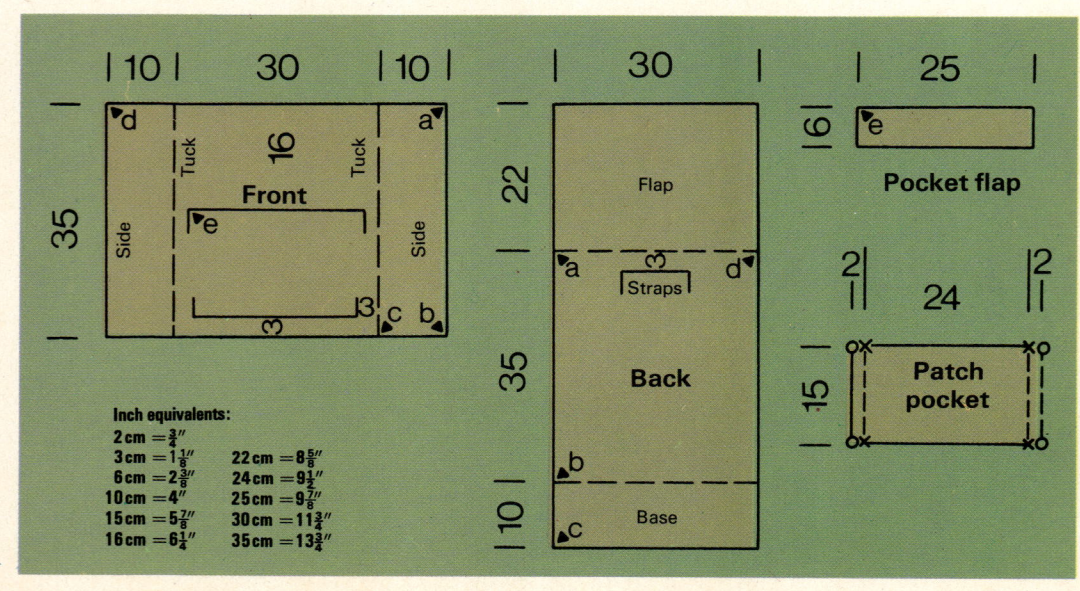

Inch equivalents:
2 cm = $\frac{3}{4}$"
3 cm = 1$\frac{1}{8}$"
6 cm = 2$\frac{3}{8}$"
10 cm = 4"
15 cm = 5$\frac{7}{8}$"
16 cm = 6$\frac{1}{4}$"
22 cm = 8$\frac{5}{8}$"
24 cm = 9$\frac{1}{2}$"
25 cm = 9$\frac{7}{8}$"
30 cm = 11$\frac{3}{4}$"
35 cm = 13$\frac{3}{4}$"

Pattern pieces are given left. Draw to measurements given. Numbers are centimeters, inches are on left.

1750

upper edge, 2 cm ($\frac{3}{4}$") from tuck, and 3 cm (1$\frac{1}{8}$") apart. On either side of flap, punch in 1 eyelet 3.5 cm (1$\frac{3}{8}$") from side and 1 cm ($\frac{3}{8}$") from lower edge.

Both packs: Turn pocket side seam allowance to inside and stitch down. Stitch tucks and stitch pocket to front, stitching through all layers at lower edge. Stitch pocket flap 1 cm ($\frac{3}{8}$") above, right sides facing, fold down, and topstitch through all layers at upper edge. Stitch back to one side down to corner, right sides facing and matching markings. Finish off seam securely and clip in straight to last stitch. Then join the side to base, and clip into seam allowance of side. Repeat on other side. Fold seam allowances in half so that raw edges are enclosed in center and stitch close to edge. Stitch tucks from right side along seams and lines marked on front.

Nylon back pack: Press under 1 cm ($\frac{3}{8}$") along a long side of the nylon tape. Place over cut edge of pack flap with the 1 cm ($\frac{3}{8}$") on wrong side and 4 cm (1$\frac{5}{8}$") on right side, mitering corners. Stitch in place. Along each side of flap, punch in tops of 3 press studs 5 cm (2") apart, placing the first one 3.5 cm (1$\frac{3}{8}$") from edge. Punch the lower parts into front, placing the first one 3 cm (1$\frac{1}{8}$") from upper edge.

Canvas back pack: Fold webbing lengthwise and press, place over flap edge, mitering corners. Stitch through all layers.

Both packs: Baste foam rubber strip onto half of one strap. Draw ring with swivel hook to center, fold strap in half, stitch together close to edge. Repeat with other strap. Baste straps to back, raw edges downward. Stitch 14 cm (5$\frac{1}{2}$") strip crosswise over the ends. Draw 18 cm (7") strips through 2 other rings. Turn in seam allowances and stitch to base.

Nylon back pack: Cut cord in half and thread through eyelets to tie at center.

Canvas back pack: Cut cord into the following lengths: 2 pieces 50 cm (19$\frac{1}{2}$") long to be sewn at center under flap corners; 2 pieces 12 cm (4$\frac{3}{4}$") long, to be drawn vertically through front eyelets and to which flap cords are tied; 2 pieces 70 cm (27$\frac{1}{2}$") long to be threaded from sides to center front. For patch pocket, 2 pieces 45 cm (17$\frac{3}{4}$") long, to be knotted into flap eyelets; 2 pieces 5 cm (2") long to be drawn through eyelets below. Pocket flap cords are tied here. Knot cords on wrong side and at other end after threading through.

This back pack is made in canvas and is fastened with cords threaded through eyelets.

All ship shape

Pack up your beach gear in a roomy canvas bag. You'll be amazed at what you can fit in, everything from your swimsuit, towel, and beach robe to all the picnic things. The bag can be carried by its shoulder straps or by a handle at one of the round ends.

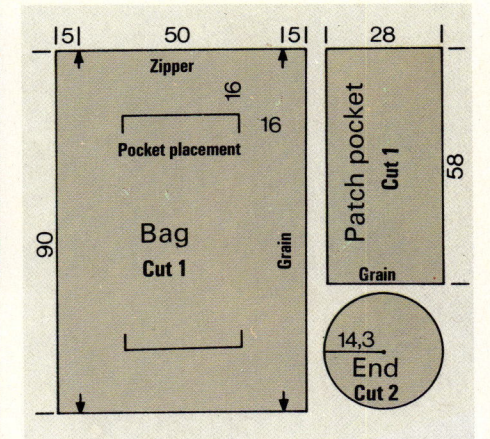

The bag has webbing handles and a separate patch pocket which goes right around. It is closed at the top by a zipper.

An extra handle is attached to one of the circular side sections so that the bag can be carried like a sailor's bag. It's the ideal bag for days on the beach and weekends by the sea.

▲ The diagram above shows the bag pieces. Make a paper pattern to these measurements:

5 cm = 2"
14.3 cm = 5⅝"
16 cm = 6¼"
28 cm = 11"
50 cm = 20"
58 cm = 23"
90 cm = 36"

Materials Required: Canvas or sailcloth: 0.95 m (1 yd), 130 cm (54") wide *or* 1.55 m (1¾ yds), 90 cm (36") wide. Webbing for handles: 2.70 m (3 yds), 5 cm (2") wide. Seam binding: 1.10 m (1¼ yds), 2 cm (¾") wide. Foam rubber for handles. Heavyweight sewing machine needle. Buttonhole thread. Zipper: 50 cm (20") long.

Cutting out: Enlarge the pattern pieces from the diagram below. Seam allowances: Add 1 cm (⅜") all around. Do not add seam allowances to the long sides of the patch pocket.
Cut webbing into 1 length of 240 cm (96") and another of 30 cm (12").

Sewing: Begin with the patch pocket. Finish the seam allowance along the narrow sides by turning to the wrong side and stitching. Pin the pocket to the bag where indicated and stitch down along the long sides. Then measure down about 20 cm (8") from each pocket top and make a line of stitching across to stop the contents from falling through.
Webbing: Press the ends back 1.5 cm (⅝"). Pin on the 240 cm (96") strip to cover the raw edges of the pocket, making sure the pressed back ends are at the bottom. Then stitch on the webbing along the 2 long sides. At the tops of the patch pocket, stitch a cross on each side to strengthen the handles (see large photograph). Then stitch the 30 cm (12") length of webbing to one of the bag ends about 4.5 cm (2") from the edge, making a strengthening cross at each handle end.
In order to give the handles a better shape and to make them more comfortable to hold, pad them with foam rubber. Cut a strip 10 cm (4") long for the end handle and 2 strips 15 cm (6") long for the other longer handles. Stitch the edges of the webbing together around the foam with zigzag stitching.
Fold the bag in half widthwise, right sides facing, and stitch the top edges together up to the zipper opening. Inside the zipper opening, cut away the seam allowance 0.5 cm (3/16"). Then finish the slit with seam binding. First stitch the binding to the bag, right sides facing, with a 0.5 cm (3/16") seam allowance, then turn to the inside, mitering the corners, and baste. Baste the zipper inside and stitch it in along the binding seam. Stitch in the circular ends and finish the raw edges.

1753

In the clear

This up-to-the-minute clutch bag, which opens to reveal a selection of pockets and loops, is designed to hold all your make-up and odds and ends in the smartest and most fashionable way.

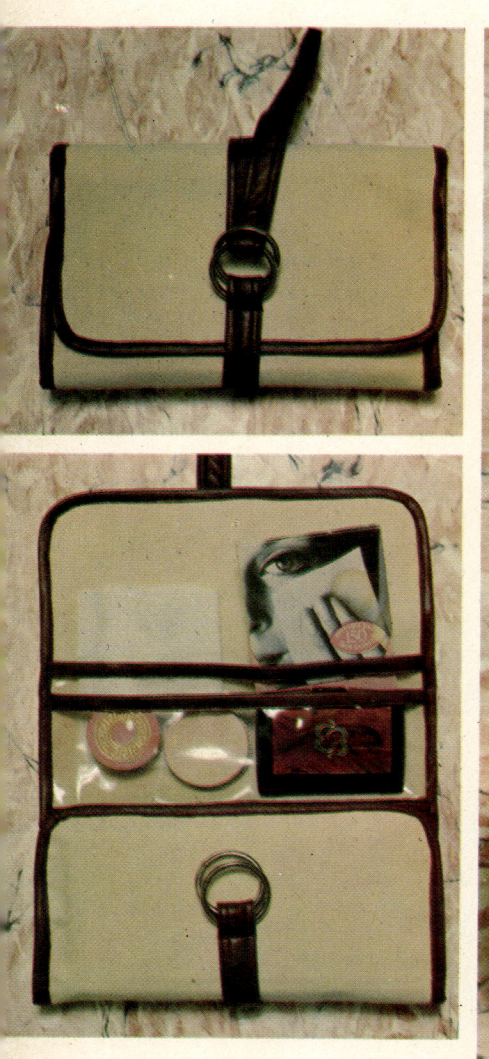

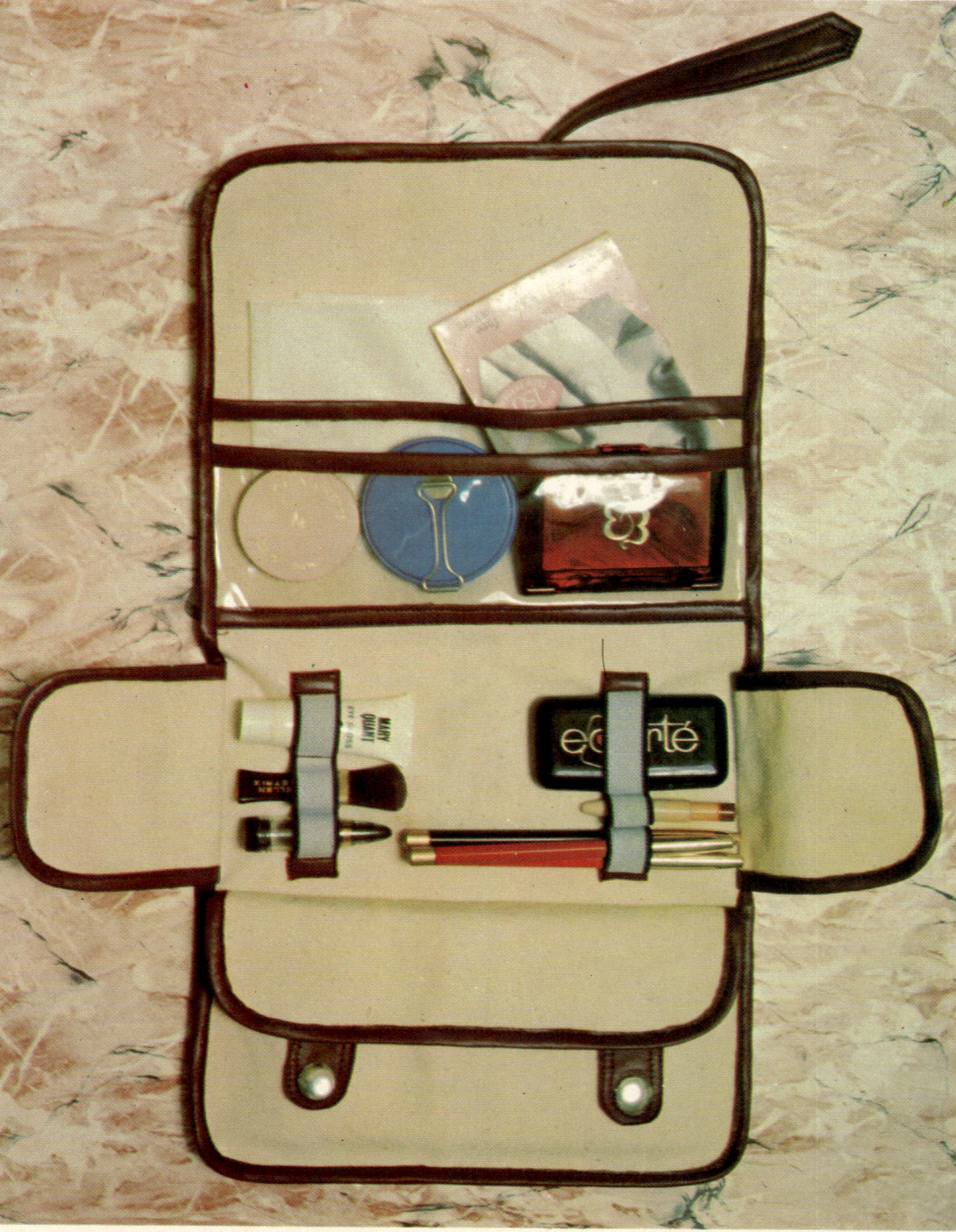

Materials Required: Canvas: 0.50 m (½ yd), 90 cm (36") wide. Synthetic leather for binding and fastening: 0.10 m (⅛ yd), 150 cm (58") wide. [In place of synthetic leather, you can use 3.10 m (3⅜ yds), 2 cm (¾") wide bias binding or braid for binding edges, and real leather or fabric for tabs and fastening.] Thick, transparent plastic for the 2 upper pockets. Elastic: 0.25 m (¼ yd), 2 cm (¾") wide. 2 punch-in press studs: 1 cm (⅜") diameter. 2 rings for the fastening: 3.5 cm (1⅜") diameter.

Cutting out: Cut out all canvas parts without seam allowance except for the pocket. Here, add 2 cm (¾") to the opening edge. Cut out the 2 upper pockets in transparent plastic. Cut out the following parts in synthetic leather: the fastening band once with 0.5 cm (¼") seam allowance; the tabs 4 times without seam allowance; for binding edges, cut 2 cm (¾") wide strips to the appropriate lengths; for each end of the elastic, a strip 2 cm (¾") wide and 1 cm (⅜") long. Cut 2 pieces of elastic 12 cm (4¾") long.

Sewing: Bind the upper edges of the plastic pockets with the synthetic leather (or binding) as follows: Fold strips in half lengthwise, fit over the edge up to the fold, and stitch close to the edge. Place the pockets together, with the lower edges level, and bind the lower edges together. Place the two together onto the main part where marked and stitch down close to lower edge. Pin on the elastic, matching points **i** and **k**. Stitch the strips of synthetic leather over the ends. Bind the curved edges of the side flaps; pin them, facing inward onto the main part, matching points **d** and **e**. Finish the top edge of the canvas pocket opening, turn the seam allowance to inside, and stitch it down. Place the tabs together in pairs, wrong sides facing, and stitch together close to edge. Bind the canvas pocket flap. Stitch the tabs under where marked. Pin this pocket (with flap attached) to the main part with the other pocket on top of it.

Bind the main part all around, catching in the side flaps and the pocket edges. Turn the seam allowances of the fastening band to the inside, fold in half lengthwise, and stitch all around, close to edge and again presser foot width away. At straight end, draw the rings through and stitch the end down. Stitch the band to the outside of the bag, matching point **h**. Finally, punch in the press studs.

Inch equivalents: 0.5 cm = ¼"; 1 cm = ⅜"; 2 cm = ¾"; 2.5 cm = 1"; 3 cm = 1⅛"; 3.5 cm = 1⅜"; 4 cm = 1⅝"; 6 cm = 2⅜"; 6.5 cm = 2⅝"; 7 cm = 2¾"; 8 cm = 3⅛"; 9 cm = 3½"; 10 cm = 3⅞"; 11 cm = 4⅜"; 12 cm = 4¾"; 21 cm = 8¼"; 23 cm = 9⅛"; 32 cm = 12⅝"; 43 cm = 16¾".

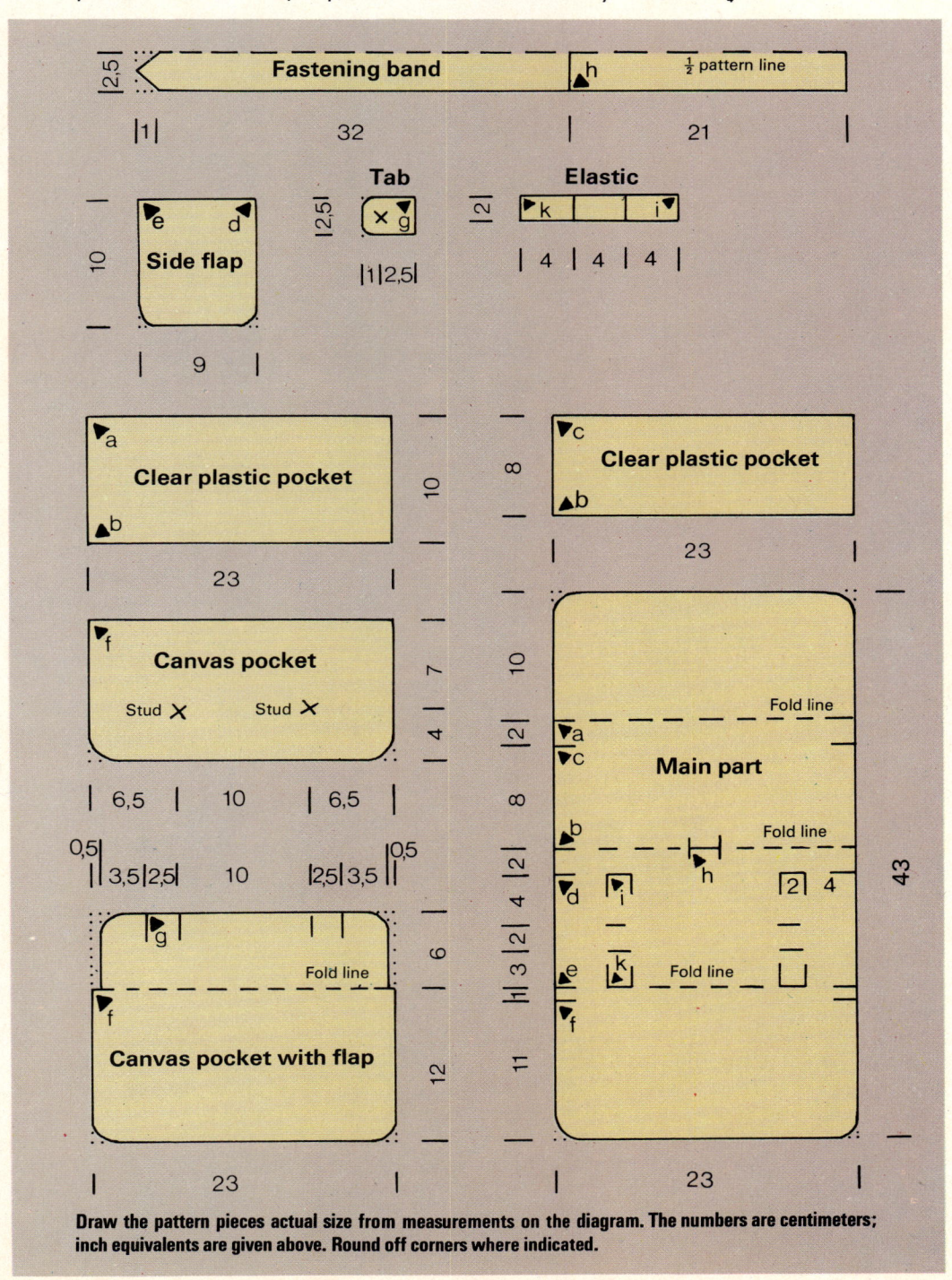

Draw the pattern pieces actual size from measurements on the diagram. The numbers are centimeters; inch equivalents are given above. Round off corners where indicated.

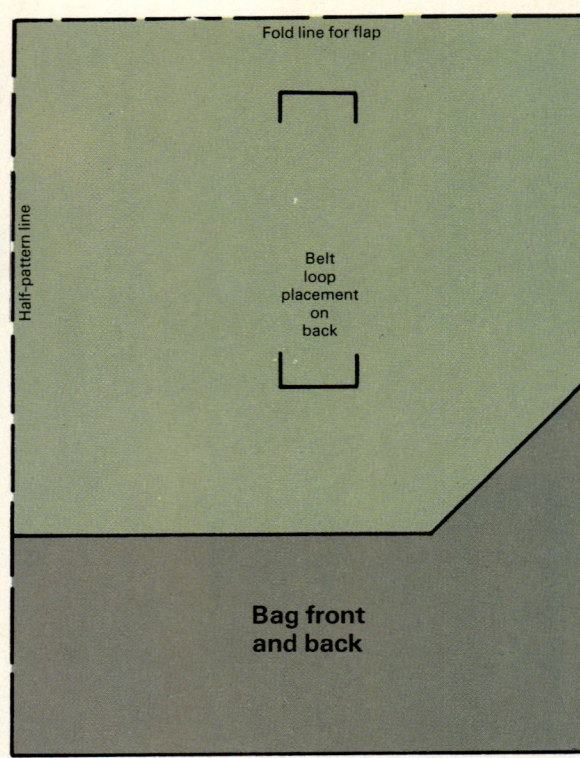

Above: The actual-size pattern shows half of the front and back of the bag plus the flap.

The small envelope-shaped bag is bound all around with a contrasting braid and it slots onto a matching belt. The back and flap are top-stitched in a diamond pattern.

Using the diagrams on the right as a guide, draw the actual-size pattern pieces onto paper.

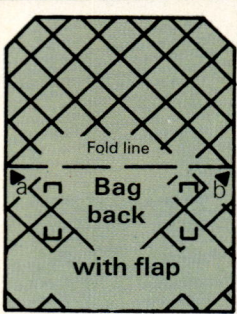

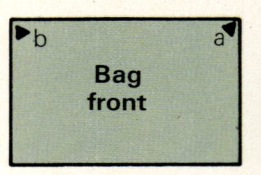

Up-to-the-minute pouch bags
Keep it hanging on

Handy little bags to wear on a narrow belt or over your shoulder are both fashionable and useful for holding money and other small items. We give you two patterns here — one for a belt bag, one for a shoulder bag. Half-patterns for each bag are given actual-size above, while the smaller diagrams show you how to fit the pieces together. You can also make the matching belt to complete the look. Use canvas or heavy cotton, which is practical and hard-wearing.

Bag with belt
Materials Required: Canvas or cotton: 0.20 m (¼ yd), 90 cm (36") wide. Braid: about 2.90 m (3⅛ yds), 2 cm (¾") wide. 1 button. 1 buckle with prong. 5 eyelets. Thread. Buttonhole twist.

Cutting out: Bag: Cut out front and back (with attached flap) once each without seam allowance, using smaller designs as a guide and larger diagram for size. Belt: Cut 1 strip 3 cm (1¼") wide and waist measurement in length, plus 20 cm (8") overlap.

Sewing: Bag: Bind upper edge of front piece with braid; to do this, press braid in half lengthwise and place over cut edge. Baste and stitch from the right side, making sure that both braid edges are caught in (leave the ends flat rather than turning them in). Now top-stitch the bag back and flap in a diamond pattern with lines 2 cm (¾") apart, using buttonhole twist.

Belt loops: Cut 2 strips of braid 5 cm (2") long, fold each in half lengthwise, stitch down and stitch to back where marked.

Now baste back to front, wrong sides facing and matching points **a** and **b**. Bind the bag base with braid as for upper edge, then bind the sides and

Pattern labels:
- Fold line for flap
- Patch pocket
- Bag front and back
- Half-pattern line

The shoulder bag has curved edges and it is also bound with braid and fastened with a button. Using the diagrams on the right as a guide, draw the actual-size pieces onto paper.

Diagram labels: Bag back with flap (Fold line, a, b, e, f); Pocket (a, b); Bag front (c, d); Gusset (c, f, d Tuck, e).

Shoulder bag

Materials Required: Canvas or cotton: 0.25 m ($\frac{1}{4}$ yd), 90 cm (36") wide. Braid: about 1.80 m (2 yds), 2 cm ($\frac{3}{4}$") wide. Twill tape: 1.10 m ($1\frac{1}{4}$ yds), 3.5 cm ($1\frac{3}{8}$") wide. 1 button. Thread.

Cutting out: Cut out the pieces widthwise on the fabric. Cut out front and back (with attached flap) and patch pocket once without seam allowance. Gusset: Cut out 1 strip 4 cm ($1\frac{5}{8}$") wide and 48 cm (19") long without seam allowance.

Sewing: Bind the upper edge of front with braid; to do this, press braid in half lengthwise and place over cut edge. Baste and stitch from the right side, making sure that both braid edges are caught in (leave ends flat rather than turning them in). Now bind the short ends of the gusset as above and stitch a narrow pin tuck about 0.2 cm ($\frac{1}{8}$") wide along the center from the wrong side. Bind the edges of the patch pocket and stitch onto flap where indicated. Now baste the front to one long side of the gusset, wrong sides facing and matching points **c** and **d**. Bind this edge, turning in braid ends. Then baste back to other side of gusset, matching **e** and **f**. Bind this edge, together with the flap. For the loop, cut a strip of braid 8 cm (3") long, fold in half lengthwise, stitch together and finish the ends. Stitch loop under center of flap. Sew on button. Finally, stitch the shoulder strap to the bag, placing it inside the top of the gusset.

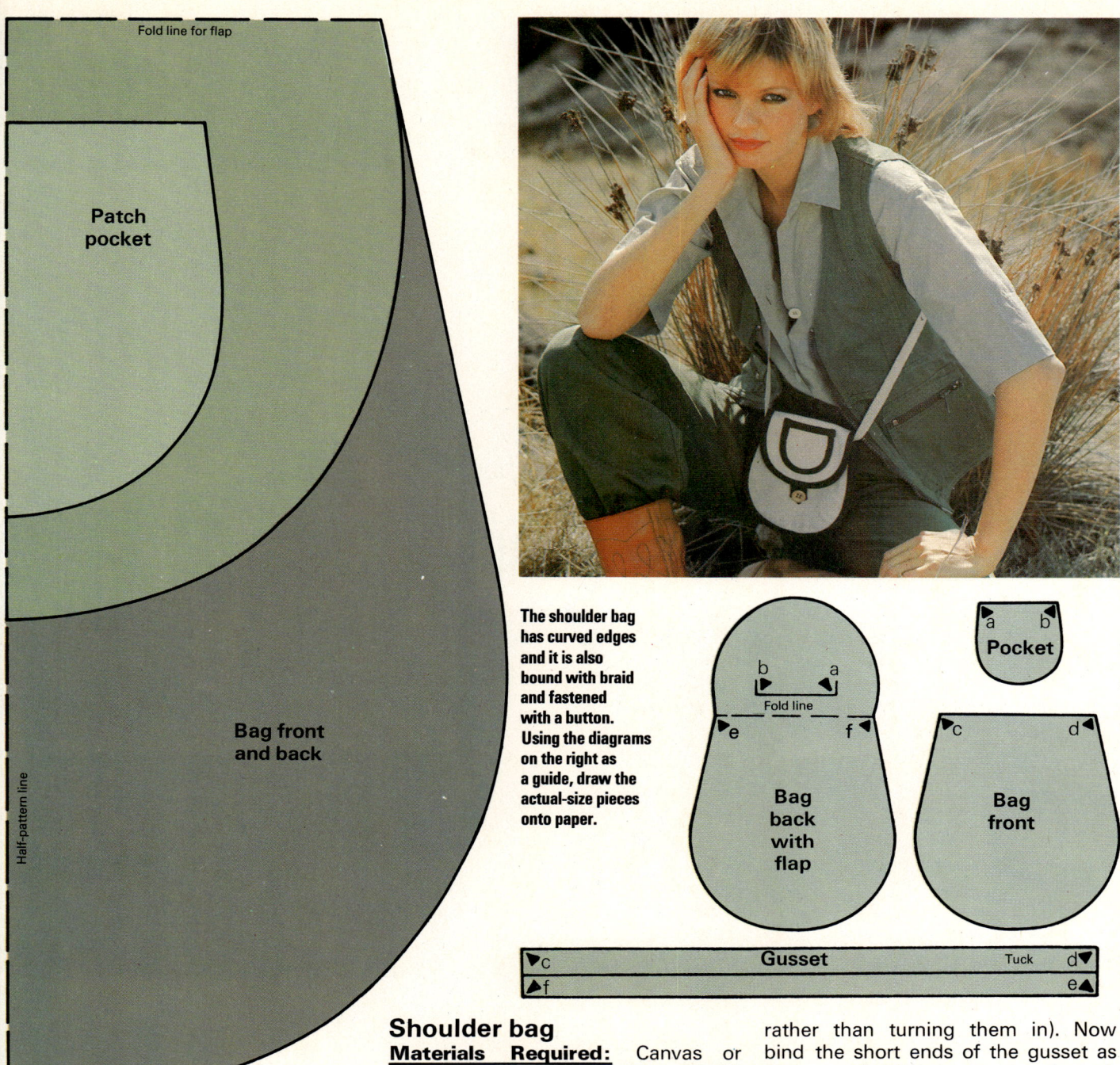

around the flap, folding in the ends here. For the braid loop, cut the braid 8 cm (3") long; fold it in half lengthwise, stitch together, and finish ends. Stitch the loop under the center of the flap. Sew on button.

Belt: Round off the corners of the overlap. Bind the fabric all around with braid as for the bag. Punch in eyelets at 6 cm ($2\frac{1}{2}$") intervals. At underlap, punch in an eyelet for the prong, draw buckle through and sew down end of belt over it.

1757

These amusing dolls are half cushion, half toy and they'll appeal to adults and children alike. They're bright, cuddly, and great fun to make. You might even like to try and invent a few more characters of your own. The pattern is given actual size on Pattern Sheet 55.

Materials Required: Suitable fabric remnants, braids, embroidery cotton, yarn, fake-fur fabric, buttons, and beads. Kapok for stuffing.

Making the cushions

The whole of the back is cut out in one piece with a 1 cm ($\frac{3}{8}$") seam allowance. For the front, trace the separate parts such as hands, face, feet, etc. from the pattern onto tissue paper, then cut out the whole front from the background fabric.

These separate pattern parts and the braids are cut out with a 1 cm ($\frac{3}{8}$") seam allowance at the outer edges; the feet, however, have a seam allowance only at the lower edge. On overlapping fabrics, take care to add a seam allowance to the underlying part, but none to the overlapping part.

The various details and trims are now appliquéd onto the background fabric, using a close zigzag stitch. To attach the narrow braids, just stitch once along the center with a straight stitch, for the wider ones, stitch along both sides.

For Dolls 2 and 3, cut out the whole of the head in one piece. Sew on the hair along the dash lines on the pattern. For Doll 2, cut 80 strands of yarn about 60 cm (23$\frac{1}{2}$") long and lay them over the head. Sew down along the dash lines with backstitch, using a strand of yarn. Braid the hair. Embroider the headband with beads (see photograph).

For Doll 3, cut 50 strands of yarn about 35 cm (13$\frac{3}{4}$") long for the hair and 100 strands about 9 cm (3$\frac{1}{2}$") long for the front. Catch in the upper ends of the short strands when you stitch the front body to the back body. Here the sewing lines for the hair are also indicated by dash lines.

When the front is finished, stitch it to the back, right sides facing, leaving the lower edge open for stuffing. Turn the doll, stuff it, then sew up the lower edge by hand.

The diagram below shows you what the pattern pieces look like. They are given actual size on the front of Pattern Sheet 55. Each head is shown separately with all of the details drawn in.

1 The traditional Tyrolean peasant is trimmed with braid and fur fabric.

2 A few fabric remnants, yarn, and beads make this colorful Indian squaw.

3 The black-haired Japanese girl has a flowered gown and a fan in her hand.

4 You'll need wool, fake-fur fabric, fabric remnants, and braid for the Eskimo.

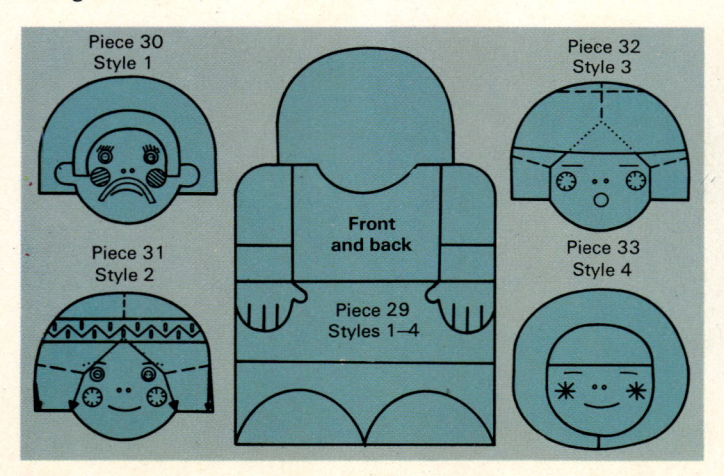

The international set

Rise and shine

Sweet dreams will be yours in these feminine nighties. The crocheted insets add a distinctive accent.

Size: Directions are for Size B (84 cm (33") bust). Changes for Size D (92 cm (36") bust) are in brackets.

Materials Required:

Crochet cotton: 50 gm or 2 oz white. Crochet hook size 1.
Fabric: 6.50 m (7$\frac{1}{8}$ yds), 90 cm (36") wide. 6 buttons.

Crocheted inset

Basic Stitch: R 1: 1 dc into 8th st from hook, * 2 ch, skip 2 ch, 1 dc in next st, repeat from * to end. **R 2:** 5 ch for turn, 1 dc in next dc, * 2 ch, 1 dc in next dc, repeat from *, working the last dc into 3rd of 5 turning ch. Repeat R 2.
For the filled-in squares, work 2 dc in place of 2 ch into ch spaces of previous R.

Tension: 13 squares = 39 sts and 16 R to 10 cm or 4".

Abbreviations: Ch = chain. Sc = single crochet. Dc = double crochet. St(s) = stitch(es). R = row(s).

Inset for Style 1: Make 86 (92) ch and work in Basic Stitch of filled-in squares for 3 (4) R. In the 4th (5th) R, begin the motif, following the chart. The white squares represent the open squares. When the 33 (35) R are completed, work an edging thus: turn corner with 1 ch, * into side edge of each square work 2 sc, then 3 ch and 1 sc into front thread of sc below (one picot formed), repeat from * all around, working a picot into each corner. Fasten off.

Inset for Style 2: Make 89 (95) ch and work in Basic Stitch of open squares for 2 (3) R. In the 3rd (4th) R, begin the motif, following the chart. The blue squares represent the filled-in squares. When 17 (19) R have been completed, work an edging as for Style 1.

Making the nighties

Cutting out: The pattern pieces are given actual-size on Pattern Sheet 54. The

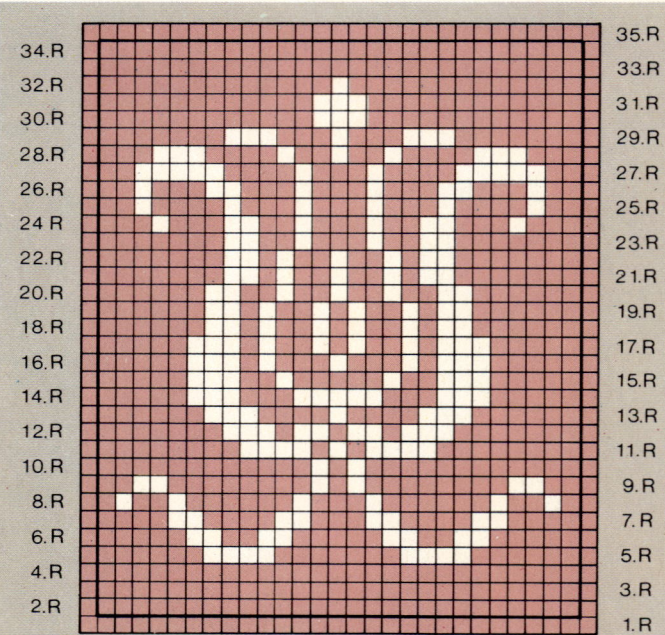

Style 1: This nightdress is pretty enough to be worn as a lounging dress during the day.

Chart for Style 1: The complete inset is shown. Pink squares represent filled-in dc squares. White squares represent open squares of 2 ch, skip 2 ch, 1 dc on dc. The heavy inner line is for the 1st size; outer outline is for the 2nd size.

Style 2: The front of this style is cut slightly higher so that it can also be worn as a long dress.

pattern pieces for the front and back of the skirt are each given in 2 parts. Trace each part separately and tape together. Seam allowances: hem 4 cm (1½"), side seams and shoulders 2 cm (¾"), elsewhere 1 cm (⅜").

Cut out the nighties following the cutting layout below.

Cut a facing strip for the back slit 5 cm x 30 cm (2" x 11¾"), plus seam allowance. For each sleeve slit, cut 1 strip 4 cm x 14 cm (1⅝" x 5½"), plus seam allowance. For the neck edge facing, shaped pieces are given. For Style 2, you will also need a stay strip for the pleats, 16 cm (6¼") long by 4.5 cm (1⅞") wide for Size B or 6.5 cm (2⅝") wide for Size D, plus seam allowances.

Sewing: On all pieces, turn under the hem allowance twice and stitch. Stitch side fronts to center along inside of pleat and finish the seam allowances together.

Stitch the front sections together from the arrow up to the crochet inset, but not into the seam allowance. At the corner, snip into the seam allowance of the side piece and press toward the side. Now press in the pleats.

Style 1: Fold pleats toward center front and baste in place at the inset edge.

Style 2: Finish the raw edges of the stay for the pleats. Fold pleats toward center front. Stitch lower ends of long edges of the stay along the stitching lines of the pleats. Baste top end to the inset edge.

Back: Stitch back sections and pleats as described for the front. Fold pleats toward center back and baste to the yoke seam.

Slit: These styles are buttoned at the back. Cut along the marked slit line. Stitch the slit facing along each side of the slit, right sides together, with 0.5 cm (¼") seam allowances, but taking as little allowance at the lower end as possible. Press the allowances toward the facing. Turn the strip to the back; fold in the raw edges. Stitch close to the edge through the seam. Stitch back yokes to back; the left-hand side ends at the facing, the right-hand side has an overlap. Finish center back edges. Join shoulder and side seams. For the neck facing, stitch the shaped strips together and finish the outer edges. At the back yoke opening, turn back the self facings, right sides together. Pin the shaped strips to the neck edge about 1 cm (⅜") in from the finished edge of the facing. Stitch all around and turn. The shaped neck strip now lies under the facing. Press the neck edge. Turn in the bottom edge of the facing and stitch along the seam.

Work the sleeve slit as described for the back slit. Join sleeve seams and gather the lower edge to cuff width. Sew on the cuff. Work buttonholes on the cuff overlap and down the back yoke. Gather the sleeve width at the armhole and set in the sleeve. Sew on buttons. Finally, sew in the crochet inset by hand or machine.

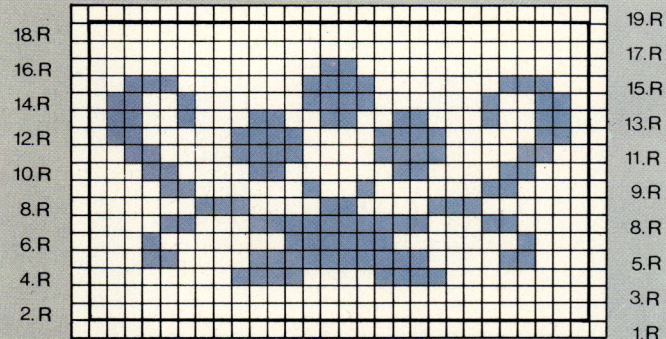

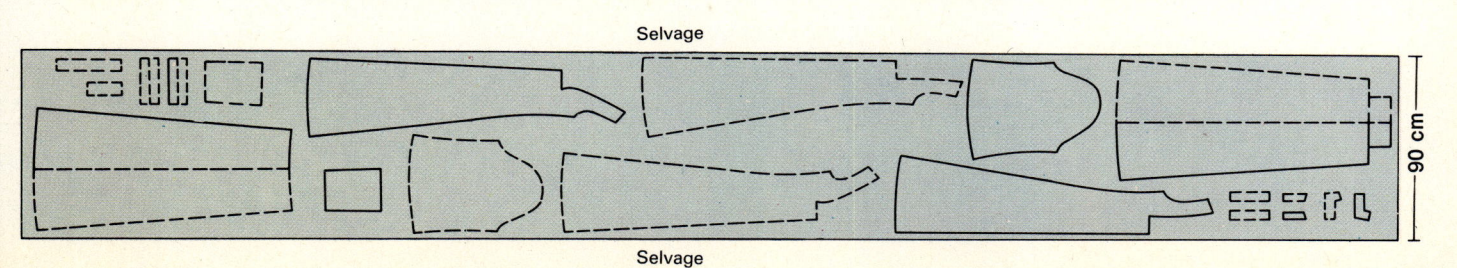

Chart for Style 2: The complete inset is shown. White squares represent open squares of 2 ch, skip 2 ch, 1 dc on dc. Blue squares represent filled-in dc squares. The heavy inner line is for the 1st size, the outer outline is for the 2nd size.

Selvage

90 cm

Selvage

1761

If you love clothes which are really individual, then this skirt is for you. Made in bright red flannel to set off the beautiful, richly-embroidered border, it's a skirt that will see you through many different occasions and win you many compliments. The style is a simple one which will not date.

Herbaceous border

The beautiful flower motif for the embroidered border is given on an actual-size pattern, so all you have to do is trace and transfer it to the skirt. The outlines are worked in chain stitch and the flowers can be filled in, if you wish, in satin stitch.

Size: B and D.
Materials Required: Sizes B and D: Flannel: 1.85 m (2 yds), 150 cm (60") wide. Grosgrain or petersham ribbon: 4 cm (1½") wide by waist measurement plus 2 cm (¾") underlap. Zipper: 20 cm (8") long. Skirt hooks.
Embroidery Materials: Stranded cotton: 18 skeins green, 8 skeins each of white and black, 6 skeins yellow.
Cutting out: The pattern piece is given actual size on Pattern Sheet 55.

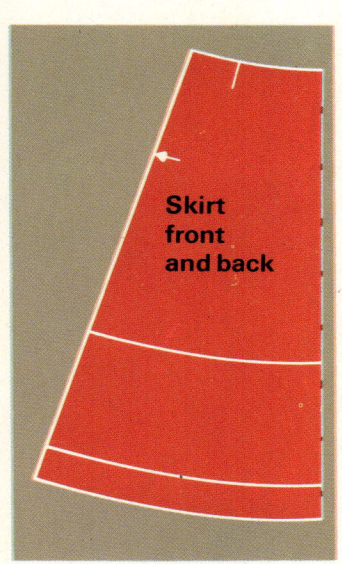

The pattern piece for the front and back of the embroidered skirt is given actual size on the reverse side of Pattern Sheet 55.

Seam allowances: add 1 cm (⅜") at the waist, 2 cm (¾") at the side seams, and 4 cm (1½") for the hem allowance. For the waistband, cut a strip 8 cm (3") wide and 70 cm (27½") long for size B or 74 cm (28¼") long for size D, plus 1 cm (⅜") seam allowance all around. Cut out the skirt from folded fabric, placing the pattern pieces one above the other on the fold.

Embroidery: Mark the center front and back, also the outlines of the embroidery area with basting thread. Join the right-hand side seam and press open. A quarter of the flower border is given on the pattern. Transfer the motif with dressmaker's carbon paper, placing it either side of center front and center back so that the border meets at the side seams. Embroider with all 6 strands of stranded cotton. All stems and leaf and flower outlines are worked in chain stitch; smaller leaves, flower calyxes, flower centers, and two of the smaller flowers are worked in satin stitch. All dots are French knots. Follow the photograph for the colors.

Sewing: Join the left side seam up to the zipper opening, taking care not to stitch over the embroidery. Finish the raw edges and stitch in the zipper. Gather the waist to the required measurement within the lines marked. Then stitch the waistband to the skirt with a 2 cm (¾") underlap. Turn up the hem and sew on skirt hooks to finish.

Skirt border

Embroider this beautiful garland of flowers in chain stitch. Join where indicated.

A

B

1765

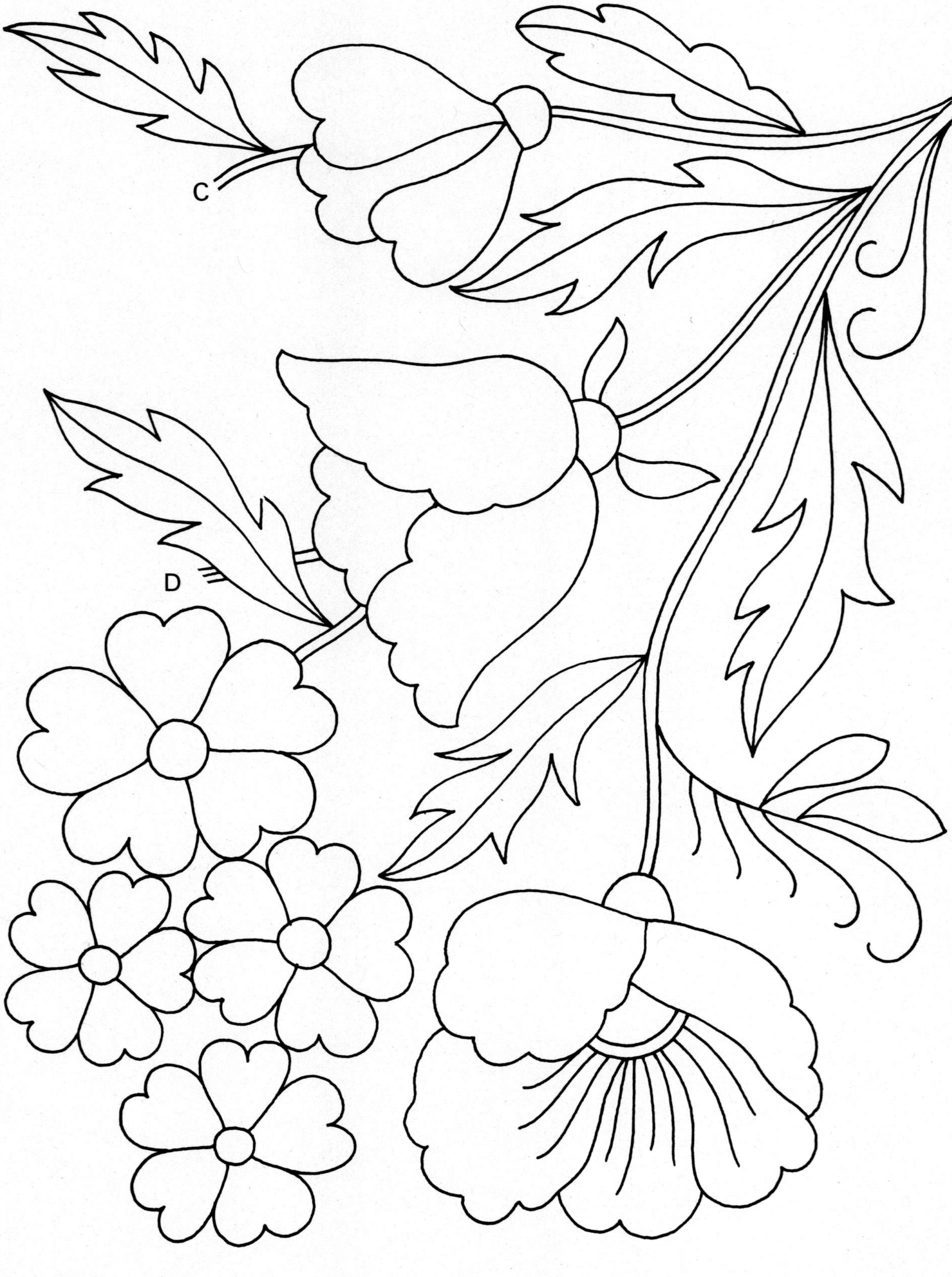
C
D

String it all together

Thread a few beads here, a tassel or two there, and in no time you'll have a set of lovely belts. Decorate a long dress or wrap one around a scarf.

Size: Each belt is about 1.95 m (2 1/8 yds) long.

Materials Required: (for each belt) 7 skeins of embroidery yarn in various colors. 64 wooden beads, 1 cm (3/8") diameter. 20 wooden beads, 0.7 cm (1/4") diameter. 2 large oval or bell-shaped beads. Narrow cotton braid. Crochet cotton for threading beads.

Making the belt

If your skeins of embroidery yarn are not ready-twisted, unwind 5 of them. Rewind each separately around a piece of cardboard 32 cm (12 1/2") long. Slip off cardboard. Hold ends taut, twist in opposite directions, and when tight, thread one end through the other. The skein will twist automatically. Wrap braid round the skeins 2 cm (3/4") from ends and stitch down. Sew 12 cm (4 3/4") lengths of crochet cotton into braid and knot together at the skein. Knot a small bead onto each end.

Thread beads between skeins as follows: draw a 30 cm (11 3/4") length of crochet cotton through the end of a skein and knot close to the skein. Thread 8 large beads onto each of the strands, knot the strands together, and draw ends through the next skein. Knot strands together well and cut threads. Repeat 4 times in all.

At ends of 2 outer skeins, thread a larger oval or bell-shaped bead. For the tassels, cut 2 different-colored skeins in half and place half of each together. Knot them onto ends of belt and wrap braid around the top to secure.

Indian style

The beadwork on this shoulder bag is based on a traditional American Indian design with its bright colors and distinctive geometric shapes.

Size: 22 cm x 18 cm (8¾" x 7⅛").

Materials Required: Lightweight canvas: 0.4 m (½ yd), 180 cm (72") wide. Rocaille beads, size 10: 2 boxes of red, 1 box each of green, yellow, white and black [1 box = about 15 gm (½ oz)]. Strong thread. Fine needle.

Bead Pattern: The chart shows ¼ of the Main Pattern, plus the complete center motif, and 1 repeat pattern of the Edge Strip. Each stroke = 1 bead.

Making the bag
Cut out the front of the bag to measurements on the diagram. Mark finished bag size (broken lines) with basting. Finish the cut edges. Mark out the beaded areas as follows: at one of the narrow sides, draw a thin pencil line 15 cm (6") long and 5.5 cm (2¼") from the edge, positioning it centrally. Draw 4 further lines each 1.25 cm (½") apart, one more 1.4 cm (9/16") away and 3 more each 1.25 cm (½") apart. These 9 lines represent the total area of the Main Pattern. At the other narrow side (upper edge), draw the edge strip 1.4 cm (9/16") wide in the same way. Begin the embroidery on the Edge Strip. Turn the bag front so that the upper edge of the bag is on the left. Bring the needle out at the upper left-hand corner, and thread up the 1st row, ie. 9 black beads. Now insert the needle again at the right-hand corner and emerge again 2–3 fabric threads lower. Thread up the next row in the opposite direction. Sew on row after row of beads in this way (see photograph). Work the 1st–17th rows once, then the 2nd–17th rows twice, then the 2nd–10th rows once, finishing with 1 row of black beads.

Embroider the Main Pattern next. It is one row shorter than the edge strip at each end. Turn the bag so the lower edge is on the left; begin at the upper left-hand corner. Embroidering the 1st pencilled strip only, work the 1st–29th rows, then in reverse, the 28th–1st rows. Begin all the following strips at the upper left-hand corner too, and embroider them close to one another. The 1st–4th strips are 8 beads wide each; the 5th one is 9 beads wide as the center bead is worked in here. Then work 3rd–1st strips in reverse.

Sewing: Cut the back of the bag the same size as the front and finish the cut edges. Turn in 4 cm (1⅝") seam allowances on front and back, making mitered corners.

For shoulder strap, cut a strip 9 cm (3½") wide and 148 cm (58") long. Join strap into a circle, press 1.5 cm (⅝") allowance to inside along the long sides and fold strip, wrong sides facing, so that edges meet at center. Pin, then stitch close to pinned edges through all layers. Baste front onto shoulder strap, edge to edge, wrong sides facing. Stitch the two parts together from right side, close to edge. Stitch back on to other side.

Cut out the front and back of bag according to the measurements on the diagram. Numbers are centimeters; inch equivalents are given below. Design areas should be pencilled in. The 9 lines of the Main Pattern are 1.25 cm (½") apart, except for the arrowed strip, where the lines are 1.4 cm (9/16") apart.

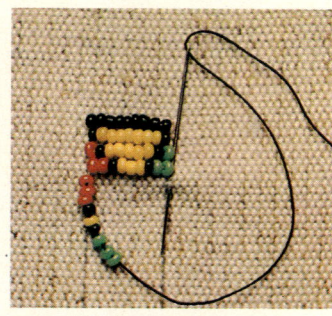

Inch equivalents:
1.25 cm = ½"
1.4 cm = 9/16"
1.5 cm = 9/16"
4 cm = 1⅝"
7.5 cm = 3"
18 cm = 7⅛"
22 cm = 8¾"

Sew bead rows singly as shown.

Beading chart: This shows ¼ of the Main Pattern (1st–4th strips) and the second half of the center motif (5th strip). 1 repeat pattern of the Edge Strip is also given. Each stroke = 1 bead in that color. Narrow black strokes = white beads. Work the strips close together.

Main pattern: 1st strip = 8 beads, 2nd strip = 8 beads, 3rd strip = 8 beads, 4th strip = 8 beads, 5th strip = 9 beads.

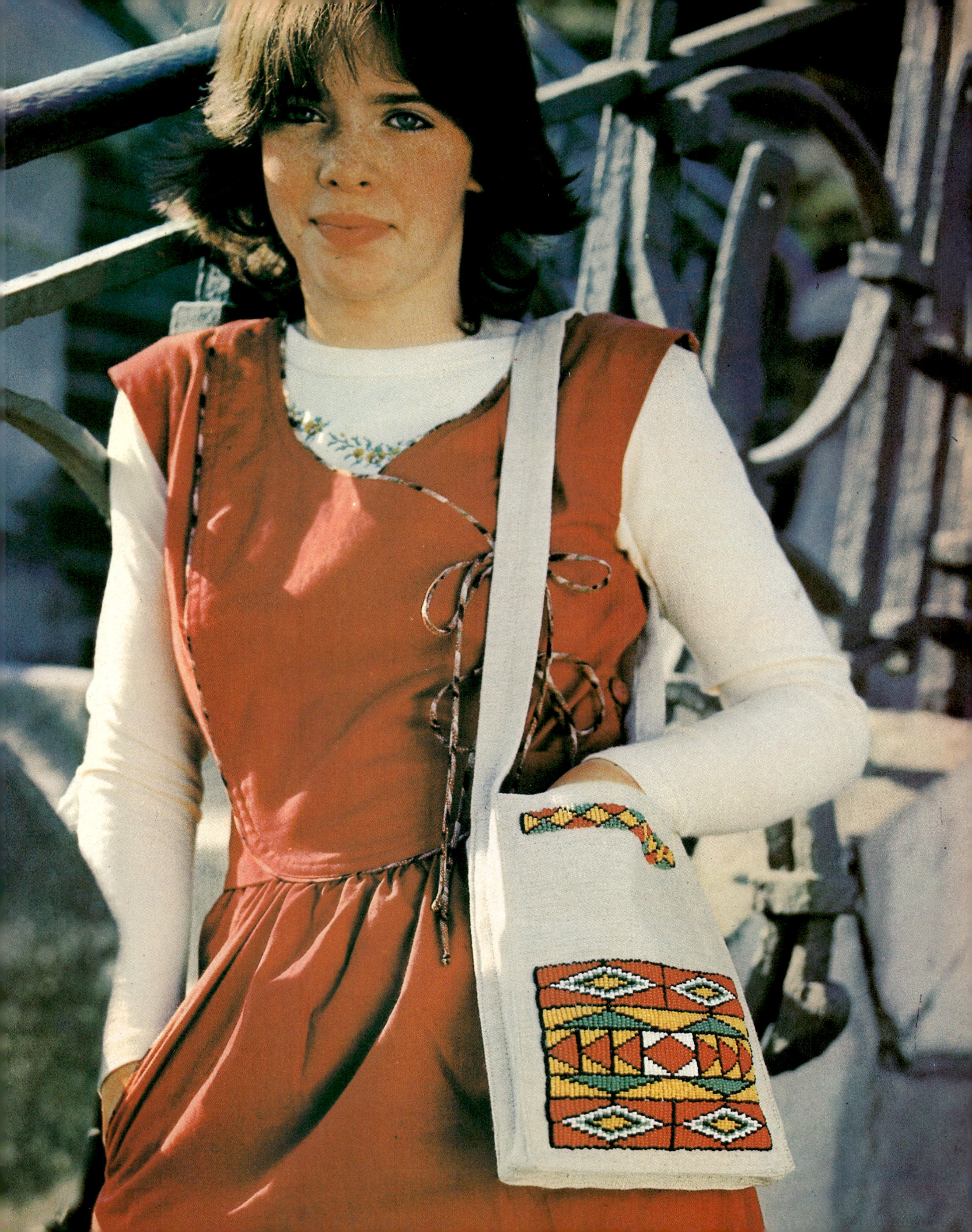

Crafts

Worked onto canvas

What a few pearls can do

Make this beaded clutch bag with its diagonal striped pattern in colors to match your favorite evening outfit. We have chosen an elegant combination of brown and white.

Size: About 15 x 27 cm (6" x 10½").
Materials Required: Piece of double canvas: 50 x 35 cm (20" x 15"), 11 or 12 holes to 2.5 cm (1"). Rocaille beads: size 10°, 150 gm or 6 oz each of white and brown *or* size 7°, 300 gm or 11 oz each of white and brown. Thick white cardboard. Remnant of brown taffeta for lining. Petersham or grosgrain ribbon for gusset: 60 cm (24"), 2.5 cm (1") wide.

Beading the bag

Draw the two sections of the bag onto the canvas, making sure that the back and front have the same number of squares of canvas. Cut out the two parts, leaving a margin of at least 2 cm (¾") all around.

Begin by beading the front of the bag in diagonal stripes, following arrows on diagram. The stripes should match up when the bag is closed. The beads are sewn to the canvas with backstitching as shown on the diagram. In the first row, work 3 brown beads, then 3 white beads alternately. In each of the following rows, stagger the pattern by one bead to the left and so on.

The size 10° beads fit exactly into each square of canvas. Slightly larger beads, such as size 7°, will fit widthways, but will be too high to fit row by row. These can be used, however, if after every 3rd row the next row of beads is worked in between two rows of canvas squares, (ie. one row of canvas is skipped).

Making up the bag

Turn the excess canvas on both sections to the wrong side. Sew ribbon gusset between front and back from points **a** along the sides and bottom to points **b**. Use small overcasting stitches, catching in the canvas threads close to the outer line of beads and the very edge of the ribbon. Cut the lining to cover the front and back/flap sections plus a 1 cm (⅜") seam allowance. Turn the bag to the wrong side and sew on the lining along the bottom and sides (not over ribbon). Leave the top edges unsewn. Turn the bag to the right side. Cut the cardboard pieces to fit the front and back sections only. Slip them inside the bag between the lining and the canvas. Slip-stitch opening.

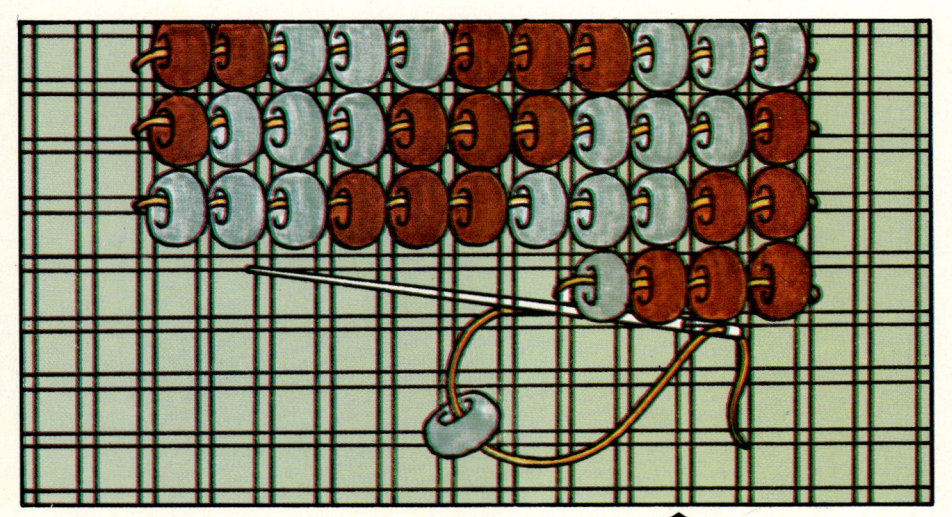

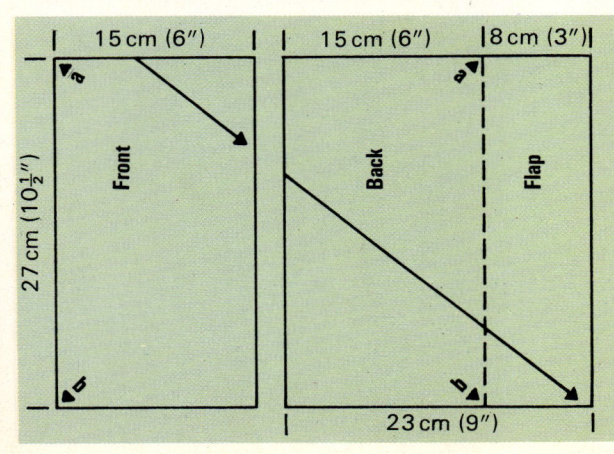

Bring the needle out through one hole, pick up a bead and reinsert the needle behind it between a pair of double threads. Bring the needle out again 2 squares further on. Continue along the row in this way.

Diagram giving the measurements of the front and back/flap sections. Direction of stripes is shown by the arrows.

1771

In contrast to the classical alphabet, this set of ornamental letters is interpreted in a very imaginative way with bead embroidery. Small, round and long bugle beads, some transparent,

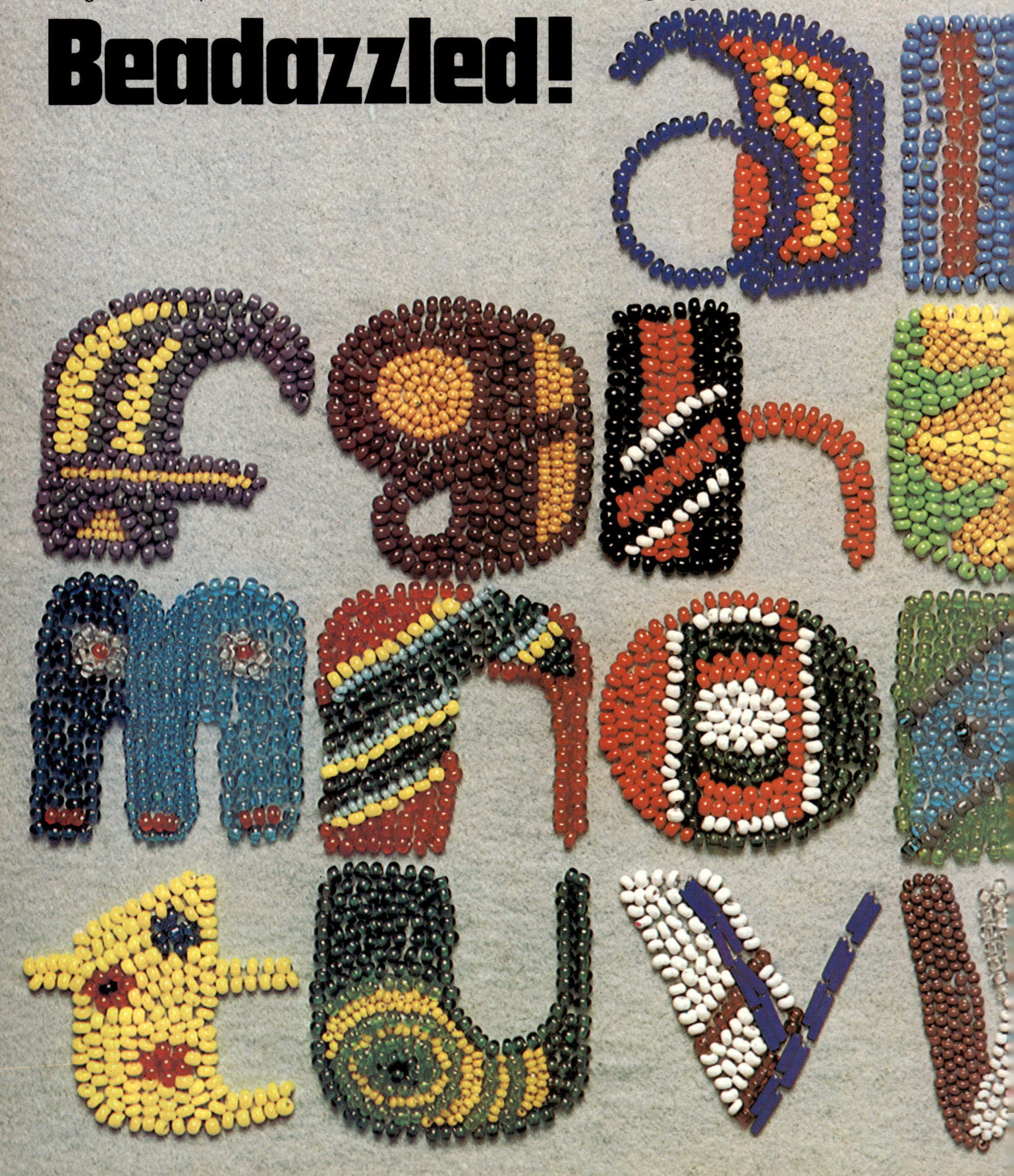

Beadazzled!

some opaque, are combined in a riot of color to form highly decorative letters. The outlines are given on a trace pattern and can be transferred with dressmaker's carbon paper.

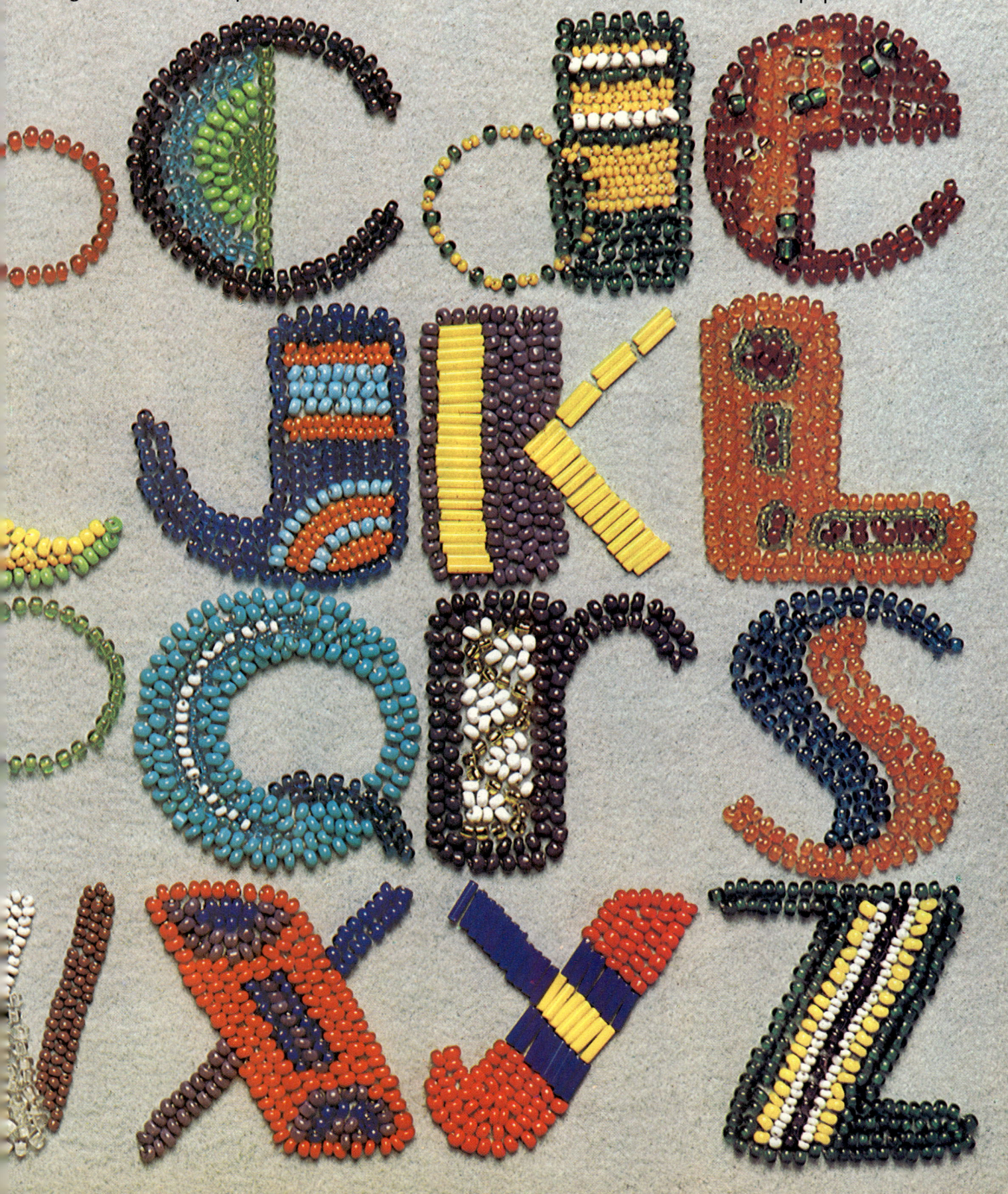

Embroidery

Our alphabet is not an ordinary one. Each letter is an ornament in its own right and can be used as a decorative initial, or built up into a name or catch-phrase. Marvellous effects can be achieved with beads — they can be transparent or opaque, large or small, round or long. Use them in blocks of color or to describe fine curving lines.

The letters can be used in many different ways. Work your own initial onto the pocket of a blouse or onto a scarf, for example. Add some glitter to your jeans with a couple of beaded letters or embroider right across the back of a denim jacket or on a tote bag.

If an item, such as a woollen pullover cannot be marked easily, trace the letters onto tissue paper, then baste the paper to the garment. Work the beading, then tear the tissue paper away afterward.

Once the letters are marked on the garment, they can be filled in as desired. Some of ours are worked with a pattern inside the letter, some are plainer. You can copy our designs or think up new ideas of your own.

Note: If you are decorating a new garment, work a practice letter first on a scrap of fabric. The base fabric should not be too thin because the beads are quite heavy when closely worked and may tear a delicate fabric.

◀ The initial C is worked here on the pocket of a silk blouse. The raised texture of the beads is effective against the textured weave of the blouse.

Embroidering with beads

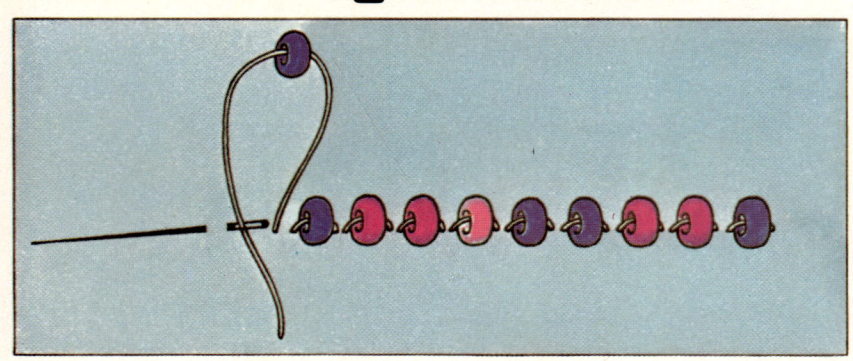

A row of round beads with running stitch

1 This is the simplest method of attaching the round beads. Thread a bead and take a short running stitch to the next bead. Continue along the row. The beads are not quite as secure with this method as with backstitch.

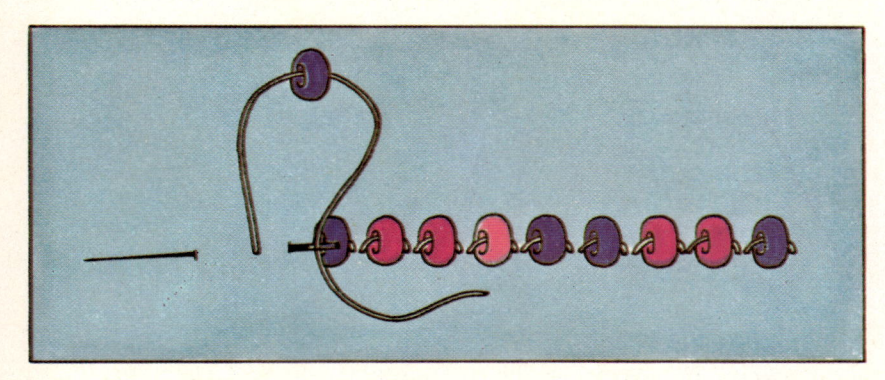

A row of round beads with backstitch

2 Here the needle is brought out one bead space further on, then the bead is threaded and the needle inserted behind it. The beads are firmer and closer than with running stitch.

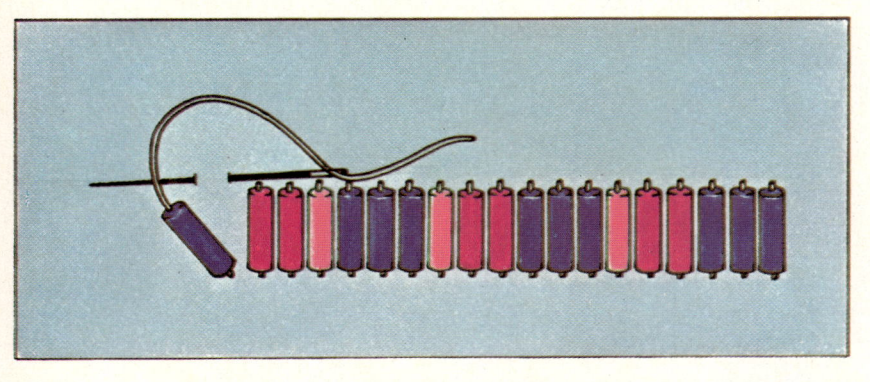

A row of bugle beads with running stitch

3 The running stitch will be worked alternately at the top and bottom of the row of beads. Thread a bead and then work a short running stitch to the top or bottom of the next bead.

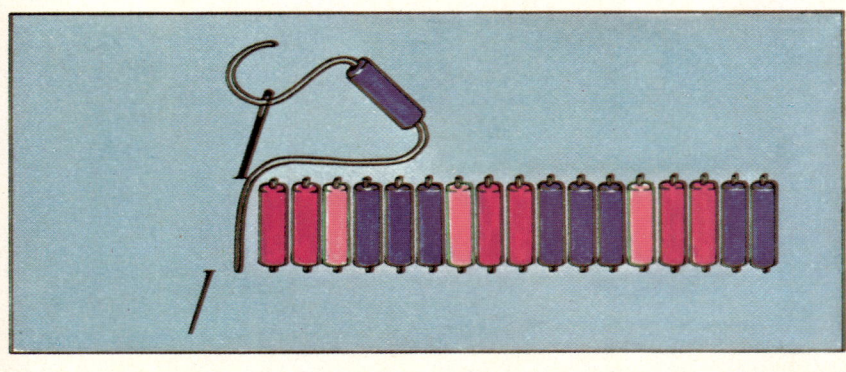

A row of bugle beads with a diagonal stitch

4 Thread a bead. Insert the needle at the top end of that bead and bring it out diagonally down at the bottom end of the next bead. This holds the beads more firmly than running stitch.

Beadwork alphabet

The letters are imaginatively embroidered with round and long beads to create a set of stunning monograms.

cdeLJKoPQ

1778

Ducks de luxe

You have probably bought dried beans and seeds for cooking and admired their lovely shapes and colors, but you may not have realised their decorative potential. You can see here how the different varieties can make an unusual ornament.

Decorating the duck
The duck is an ordinary plastic decoy duck available from sports shops. You will also need clear glue and as wide a variety of beans and seeds as you can find. Look in grocers' shops and delicatessens — kidney beans, haricot beans, butter beans, black-eyed beans, dried green beans, split peas, lentils, sunflower seeds, and chick peas are all suitable.

Spread glue thickly over the duck, section by section, and arrange beans of a suitable shape and size in rows, following the shape of the duck. Make adjacent areas contrast as much as possible for a striking effect. Leave the duck to dry well.

1779

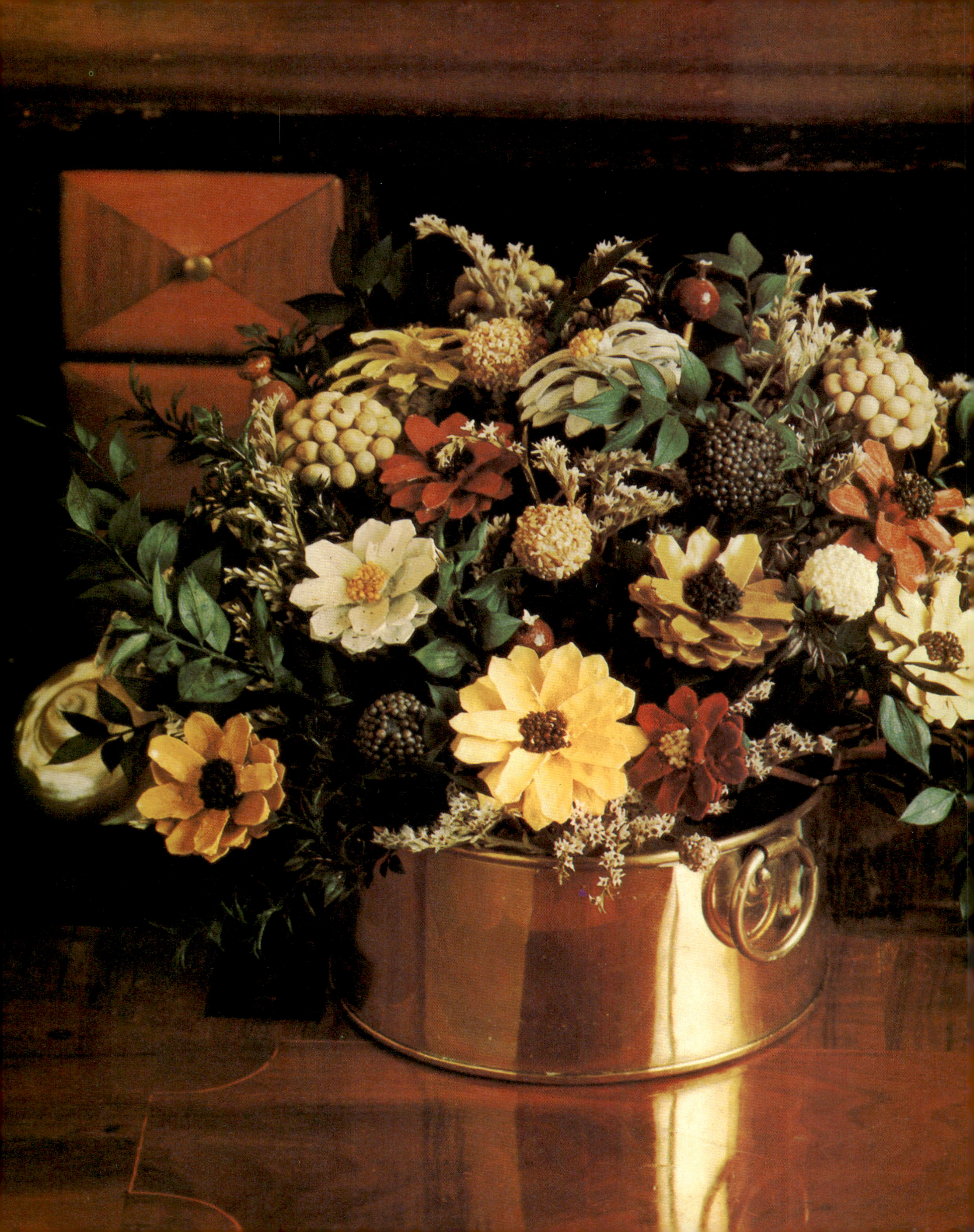

Pick of the bunch

Our impressive floral centerpiece will never wither or fade as the "flowers" are made of painted pine cones interspersed with a variety of dried grasses, seed heads, thistles, and evergreen leaves.

Materials Required:

Container. Polystyrene to fill container. Glue. Poster paint in white and a variety of colors. Clear varnish. Pine cones. Cutters to halve pine cones. Small seeds, dried seed heads, grasses, thistles. Absorbent cotton balls. Wooden kebab sticks.

Making the bouquet

Choose a suitable container. You may wish to use a basket, earthenware pot, or brass bowl (the latter must be painted with a thin coat of varnish to avoid tarnishing). Fill the container with layers of polystyrene cut to size (photograph 1) and glue it down around the edge. Paint the surface of the top layer in a dark color (see photograph 6). For the flowers, you will need some well-dried pine cones. Halve these across the center with cutters (photograph 2). The lower, wide part is used for the flowers. Drill a hole through from the bottom and insert a painted wooden kebab stick as a stem. Glue firmly. Dip the flowers into thinned white paint and leave to dry well. Then dip them into colored paint, mixed as desired (photograph 3). If a cone closes up again after painting, put it into the oven to dry it out until it reopens.

Cover the center of each flower with glue and sprinkle it with small seeds. Alternatively, paint it in a contrasting color. Finally, spray some of the flowers lightly with clear varnish, leaving others matt for contrast (photograph 4).

When making up the bouquet, work from the center outwards, positioning the center flowers higher than the surrounding ones for a well-balanced effect.

Fill in the spaces with dried seed heads, dried grasses, and thistles. You can also glue small balls of absorbent cotton onto kebab sticks, dip them into paint, and decorate with small acorns or cloves (photograph 5). Or cover with glue and dip into poppy seeds or mustard seeds. Another idea is to halve larger balls of cotton and glue dried peas onto them.

For the finishing touch, add green or dark red evergreens to the bouquet, placing them among light-colored dried flowers.

1 First choose a suitable container such as a brass bowl and line it with layers of polystyrene cut to fit the shape exactly.

2 For the flowers, you will need the lower halves of some well-dried pine cones. Cut them through the center.

3 Stick the flower shape onto a painted kebab stick and dip into thinned white paint. When dry, dip into colored paint.

4 To add interest to the bouquet, spray some of the flowers with a clear varnish, leaving others matt.

5 Other decorations include cotton balls glued onto kebab sticks and dipped into poppy or mustard seeds.

6 When arranging the bouquet, work from the center toward the outside, with the central ones higher than the rest.

How-to

Painting plastic flowers

1 Assemble the materials above. Use enamel paint.

2 These and many other plastic flowers are available from large stores. The more varieties you use, the lovelier the bouquet will be.

3 Cut off all the leaves along the stem. Leave the sepals.

4 Each bloom needs a stem. Add wire stems if necessary.

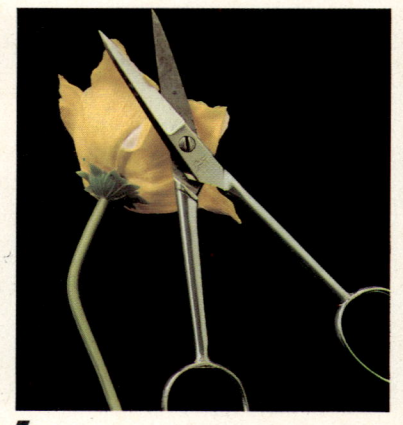

5 Trim any ragged edges of the petals with scissors.

6 Take composite flowers apart and paint each part singly.

7 Mix the colors on the plate. Pastel shades are made with large amounts of white. Paint the stems and sepals green.

Crafts

Summer flowers for a winter bouquet

*M*ake elegant arrangements or informal bouquets with plastic flowers painted in soft colors and dried grasses or evergreen leaves.

1

2

3

4

5

A cut above the others

Transform any plain surface into a riot of color with the art of découpage. The designs are made up of a number of cut-out shapes which are then pasted down, varnished, and sandpapered until the paper is embedded in the layers of varnish and a beautifully smooth surface appears. We have decorated everyday objects such as a tray, a pillbox, a tea caddy, a face-cream jar, and other small boxes.

We have used one of the examples from the previous pages to illustrate the technique of découpage.

Materials Required: Tin or plastic container or tray. Wet-and-dry sandpaper. Colored spray paint. Small, sharp scissors. Paper paste or glue. Colored prints or magazine illustrations. Brush and clear varnish.

*

First sandpaper the article thoroughly and spray with paint. Then decide on the theme for the decoration and choose the prints or the magazine illustrations.

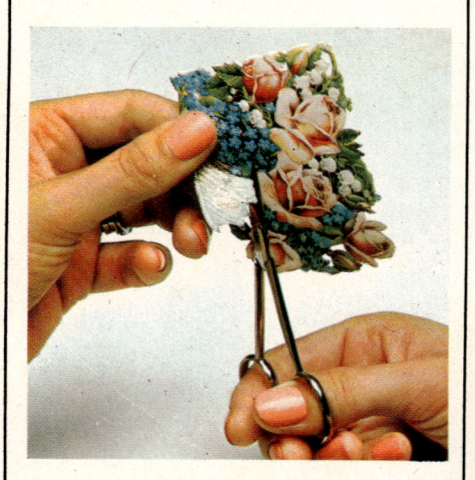

Cut them out very precisely, carefully cutting close to the flower petals and stems and taking care not to cut right through any fine lines. Cut larger motifs according to the size of the item you are covering. Alternatively, cut out smaller motifs to be grouped as a larger motif. Arrange the motifs, moving them around until the most pleasing pattern is formed before sticking them down. Take your time over this preliminary planning. Don't start until the design is planned.

If using magazine illustrations, test-glue a scrap to be sure the printing on the other side of the paper won't show through.

Now spread paste on the underside of the motifs one by one, working on a sheet of paper. You need to change the work surface often to prevent the face of the scraps from sticking to it and tearing as you lift them off.

Always stick on the motifs from the outside to the inside or, on larger surfaces, from one side to the other. If you want the base color to show, arrange the motifs with spaces between. Otherwise, make a solid cover by placing them so that they overlap slightly.

Stick an especially attractive motif over the final space. Make sure that the paste has reached right to the edge of the motifs. Test them afterward and, if necessary, spread some more paste under the edges. Remove any paste stains with a damp cloth. Any torn areas can be touched up with a felt-tipped pen.

Finally, coat the whole surface with a colorless varnish. Leave to dry thoroughly and then sandpaper it. Repeat the varnishing and sanding process, building up layers of varnish until a completely smooth and hard-wearing surface is achieved.

Index

Afghan crochet
   embroidery on   1721
   jacket, child's   1720

Alphabet, beaded   1772

Back pack, sewn   1750

Bag
   beaded   1768, 1770
   sewn   1746, 1749, 1750, 1752, 1754, 1756

Bathrobe, sewn
   child's   1736
   man's   1736
   woman's   1736

Beading
   alphabet   1772, 1774
   bag   1768, 1770
   belt   1767
   embroidery   1775

Belt, beaded   1767

Body measurements chart   1673

Bolero, woman's
   knitted   1680
   sewn   1746

Cardigan, knitted
   child's   1694, 1702
   woman's   1675

Centimeter
   conversion to inches   1672
   ruler   1673

Children
   afghan crocheted jacket   1720
   bathrobe, sewn   1736
   cardigan, knitted   1694, 1702
   culottes, sewn   1742
   dirndl jacket, knitted   1690
   doll, sewn   1758
   dress
      knitted   1700
      sewn   1726
   dungarees, sewn   1726, 1744
   hat, sewn   1726
   jacket
      crocheted   1720
      knitted   1690
      sewn   1744
   pants, sewn   1740
   pullover
      crocheted   1715, 1716, 1718
      knitted   1696, 1698, 1702

   skirt
      knitted   1702, 1704
      sewn   1746
   tank top, knitted   1692
   toy doll, sewn   1758

Clutch bag
   beaded   1770
   canvas   1754

Collar, sewn shawl   1738

Crafts
   beading
      bag   1768, 1770
      belt   1767
      monogram patterns   1776, 1778
      monograms   1772, 1774
   découpage   1784
   painting plastic flowers   1782
   pine cone flowers   1780
   seed craft   1779

Crochet
   afghan crochet
      child's jacket in   1720
      embroidery on   1721
   flowers   1711
   leaves   1711
   loop   1712
   panel   1760
   pillow   1709, 1712
   place mat   1714
   pullover
      child's   1715, 1716, 1718
      woman's   1716
   shawl, woman's   1706, 1708

Culottes, child's sewn   1742

Cushion—see Pillow

Découpage   1784

Dirndl jacket, knitted
   child's   1690
   woman's   1688

Doll, sewn   1758

Dress
   child's
      knitted   1700
      sewn   1726
   woman's sewn   1728

Dressmaking—see Sewing

Dungarees, child's sewn   1726, 1744

Embroidery
   afghan crochet, on   1721
   bead   1775
   skirt   1762

Fabric
   lace, cutting and stitching   1730
   permanently pleated, stitching   1731

Flowers
   crocheted   1711
   painted plastic   1782
   pine cone   1780

Hat, sewn
   child's   1726
   woman's   1746

Illustrated Sewing—see also Sewing

Illustrated Sewing 53   1722

Illustrated Sewing 54   1728

Illustrated Sewing 55   1732

Illustrated Sewing 56   1736

Inch
   conversion to centimeters   1672
   ruler   1672

Jacket
   child's
      crocheted   1720
      dirndl   1690
      sewn   1744
   woman's
      dirndl   1688
      knitted   1678
      sewn   1722

Knitting
   bolero, woman's   1680
   cardigan
      child's   1694, 1702
      woman's   1675
   dirndl jacket
      child's   1690
      woman's   1688
   dress, child's   1700
   jacket, woman's   1678
   openwork pattern   1694
   picot edging   1677
   pullover
      child's   1696, 1698, 1702
      woman's   1684, 1686

Index

shawl, woman's 1682
skirt, child's 1702, 1704
tank top, child's 1692
vest, woman's 1683, 1686

Lace, cutting and stitching 1730

Measurements chart, body 1673

Measurements, conversion of 1672

Men's bathrobe, sewn 1736

Metric
conversion 1672
ruler 1673

Monograms, beaded 1772, 1774

Nightgown, woman's sewn 1760

Painting plastic flowers 1782

Pants, child's sewn 1740

Pattern Sheet 53—children's clothes; suits, woman's
adapting for additional sizes
body measurements chart

Pattern Sheet 54—evening dresses, woman's
adapting for additional sizes
body measurements chart

Pattern Sheet 55—culottes, girl's; shirts, woman's
adapting for additional sizes
body measurements chart

Pattern Sheet 56—bathrobes for all the family; short & long pants, boys
adapting for additional sizes
body measurements chart

Picot edging, knitted 1677

Pillow
crocheted 1709, 1712
sewn 1758

Place mat, crocheted 1714

Pleated fabric
dress 1728
stitching 1731

Pullover
child's
crocheted 1715, 1716, 1718
knitted 1696, 1698, 1702

woman's
crocheted 1716
knitted 1684, 1686

Sewing
back pack 1750
bag 1746, 1749, 1750, 1752, 1754, 1756
bathrobe
child's 1736
man's 1736
woman's 1736
bolero, woman's 1746
canvas bag 1752
collar, making a shawl 1738
culottes, child's 1742
doll 1758
dress
child's 1726
woman's 1728
dungarees, child's 1726, 1744
fabric
lace, cutting and stitching 1730
permanently pleated, stitching 1731
hat
child's 1726
woman's 1746
jacket
child's 1744
woman's 1722
lace, cutting and stitching 1730
nightgown, woman's 1760
pants, child's 1740
pillow 1758
pleated fabric, stitching 1731
shirt, woman's 1732
shorts, woman's 1746
skirt
child's 1746
woman's 1722, 1746, 1762
suit, woman's 1722
toy, doll 1758
yoke, inserting 1734
zipper, concealed coat 1724

Shawl collar, sewn 1738

Shawl, woman's
crocheted 1706, 1708
knitted 1682

Shirt, woman's sewn 1732

Shorts, woman's sewn 1746

Sizing, fashion 1673

Skirt
child's
knitted 1702, 1704
sewn 1746
woman's
embroidered 1762
sewn 1722, 1746, 1762

Suit, woman's sewn 1722

Tank top, child's knitted 1692

Tassel belt 1767

Toy doll, sewn 1758

Vest, woman's knitted 1683, 1686

Women
bag
beaded 1768, 1770
sewn 1746, 1749, 1750, 1752, 1754, 1756
bathrobe, sewn 1736
belt, beaded 1767
bolero
knitted 1680
sewn 1746
cardigan, knitted 1675
dirndl jacket, knitted 1688
dress, sewn 1728
hat, sewn 1746
jacket
knitted 1678
sewn 1722
nightgown, sewn 1760
pullover
crocheted 1716
knitted 1684, 1686
shawl
crocheted 1706, 1708
knitted 1682
shirt, sewn 1732
shorts, woman's 1746
skirt
embroidered 1762
sewn 1722, 1746, 1762
suit, sewn 1722
vest, knitted 1683, 1686

Yarn, selecting 1672

Yoke, inserting 1734

Zipper, concealed coat 1724

Notes

Notes

Notes

Notes